Choosing Joy
in the Midst of Crisis

Dolly Mae

Hara Publishing Group

Choosing Joy in the Midst of Crisis

Dolly Mae

Published by
Hara Publishing Group
P.O. Box 19732
Seattle, WA 98109
(425) 775-7868

ISBN: 1-883697-54-9
LCCN: 2002107669

To Contact the Author:
If you would care to comment on this book, or if you would like a complete description of Dolly's workshops and how to arrange for them:
E-mail Dolly Mae at dolly@dollymae.com
Web: www.dollymae.com

or send a self-addressed envelope to:

Dolly Mae
22833 Bothell Everett Hwy., Suite 102-1288
Bothell, WA 98021

Printed in the United States
10 9 8 7 6 5 4 3 2

Table Of Contents

Dedication

I lovingly dedicate this book to Rajni,
my teacher of unconditional love.

Acknowledgments and Special Thanks

Support on my journey has been awesome and I would like to thank:

Jim Jenkins, my unconditionally loving sweetheart,
life partner and best friend;

Eric Braff, an extraordinary spiritual graphic artist
and the cover designer;

Jen McCord, who first told me I was a good writer,
and made me believe it;

Susan Lamont, who suggested that the triangles
would be worth writing a book on.

Chapter 1

My Story

How I Came to Write This Book

At age five I realized the church didn't have all the answers when the Monsignor teaching our religion class was stumped by a little girl. She had asked a most reasonable question, "If everything God created is good, why are there rats?"

Our esteemed teacher verbally attacked the girl, shouting at her to stop asking such ridiculous questions and sit down immediately. In that moment I knew my connection to the Catholic church was broken and felt that from then on if I wanted answers, I'd have to look elsewhere. That search led me through many religious and philosophical systems and brought me to the information I present to you in this book.

In college I wound up designing my own curriculum. It crossed many disciplines and concluded with a thesis on the origin and development of myth and folklore. Although I didn't know it then, this was my introduction to the field that occupies me now. Many of you will recognize the extensive field of endeavor as it relates to the incomparable Joseph Campbell.

I had joined the Army and met my husband there. Our partnership launched the business we built together. He had always had a passion for investing and I remember the day he came home excited about a three-unit building he'd seen for sale. He told me the details and I said, "Do you mean that after paying all the expenses including the down payment we'd still have $50 a month profit?" He said yes and I replied, "Why wouldn't we!" So we did. Sixteen years and a $25 million real estate empire later, we declared bankruptcy, but more about that shortly.

By 1979 soaring interest rates and balloon payments had destroyed the sensible purchases of apartment buildings. I decided that if we switched to buying one rental home a month— which was easier but had always seemed a waste of time to me—it would be equivalent to buying a 12-unit building a year. In the end we owned 350 houses and 300 apartment units.

This also led to other businesses. Since many houses needed rehab and all needed upkeep, we bought a small cleaning company. Within two years it had grown nearly 15 times and we were cleaning everything from private homes to the local brewery. Then I got a general contractor's license and soon had 52 full-time subcontractors on 40 sites. I loved all the juggling, management, hiring, training, financing. I had such a positive attitude that I didn't have the fear of debt many people have. I spoke to investment groups and taught others how to do the same thing I did.

Crisis

Our business was growing rapidly with no end in sight when suddenly the bottom fell out of financing for rental properties. Overnight the funding pools dried up due to the multimillion dollar fraud of a con artist investor in California and the subsequent severe over reaction of FannyMae, FreddyMac, and FHA. On top of that, drug gangs were moving into the inner-city areas I specialized in, causing tenants to move out and values to plummet.

After 264 loan rejections, I'd finally found a Savings and Loan to refinance my portfolio. The result would have been a substantial monthly cash flow, all debts paid and two million dollars in cash reserves. I felt all the hard work would finally pay off and we would have retired after surmounting a final enormous obstacle. Just prior to loan closing, the lender was taken over by the Federal Government and shut down. My last hope died away. For seventeen years I'd had perfect credit with 700 mortgages and never a late payment, but within 30 days all that was destroyed with my first ever late payment and the bloodletting began. It was an unimaginable nightmare.

Turning Point

As the crisis was building, I decided to give my thoughts a break by reading a book, something completely unrelated to what was happening. I remembered my sister mentioning Edgar Cayce, so I checked *There is a River* by Thomas Sugrue out of the library. It was fascinating but nothing more, I thought, until I reached the end of the book and found a section called "Philosophy," which I later learned *is not in every edition.* I read it and was blown away. There were actually people out there who thought like me. Where there was one, there had to be more and this sparked a reading frenzy, fueled by my disintegrating "real world", as I zipped through 450 books in one year. The passion and intensity in my finding this support was comparable to finding a soulmate.

Halfway through this frenetic reading, I saw in a local metaphysical newspaper that a teacher named Rajni would be speaking near my home. Wasn't that synchronous? (One of my new words.) I attended and was hooked. It so fed my soul that something in me changed forever. I had been dying of thirst and it was like pure, cold, crystal clear water. Here was someone of whom I could ask questions, interrogate, argue, discuss and learn. I started coming once a week, then every day, then practically around the clock while Rajni was "in residence" in my area.

Eventually I had learned not only a different way to think regarding just about everything, but a completely different - and much more joyful - way to live my life. I admit I was desperate—for one thing I had been seriously considering suicide—but the tools I seized to survive my catastrophe became a lifetime method not to avoid that or any other crisis in future, but simply to choose joy instead.

This book is the story of what I learned in that five months that so changed my world and of what I teach others that they too may survive their own life crises and remember to choose joy in the very next moment.

As I got fed with my new way of thinking, feeling and living, I began teaching others, at first in psychic readings and later in weekly classes. Even as the lengthy workout bankruptcy proceeded over a seven-year period, I was finding considerable joy with my newfound career. I attended large international psychic fairs and lectured all over the world in Greece, Peru, Hawaii, the Caribbean, Bali and Canada. Even in the midst of my 'crisis' I was having full time joy.

Since that time I have learned to live this way - by choosing joy. The biggest help has been the toolkit of information and personal growth techniques I've assembled which I pass along to you here.

Choose joy. It works.

Chapter 2

Creating Our Reality

How Do We Create What Happens to Us?

We are already creating our reality whether we know it or not. Therefore we can avoid creating a reality we don't enjoy simply by learning the process and taking charge of it. At the highest level of our beings, we haven chosen our names, our families, our DNA patterning and our general circumstances before birth. It is a function of our creator aspect, our highest level of awareness, which precedes, runs concurrent with, and will still exist after our human experience.

To consciously determine the outcome of our self-creative process, we must first decide we want to create differently and then believe we can. As we begin to see how we have created particular circumstances and situations, we can take ownership of our own powerful creative ability beginning the long journey out of the pit of victimhood, rung-by-rung, step-by-step, up to the light of self-empowerment. We can redirect our power in a healthy, more joy-filled way.

Many times things do not seem to be going right in our lives. One danger of accepting ourselves as the "creator" of negative experiences is using them to beat ourselves up. "How dumb can I be? How could I have been so blind?" "How could I have screwed up so badly?" Instead we can see ourselves as powerful originators of our own life experiences. If we can make such enormous messes, we can surely create dynamic successes. At this point, our self worth is critical. Do we see ourselves as capable or worthy of making such changes? Can we access our own power? Remembering who we really are is essential to this decision. Knowing ourselves as aspects of God, we can.

As my business was crashing, I didn't understand why, but I already knew enough to ask my question this way: "Why did I create this disaster?" instead of "Why has this happened to me?" as if I weren't its creator when clearly, according to the new principles I was learning, I was. Yes, the bank had been closed, but why had I created *being there then*? Asking what was going on in this way was empowering. It was the basis for seeing that I was creating and could do it differently from then on.

We came to this reality in the first place to *remember,* not to learn anything new, but to remember that we *are love* and to play the game of pretend, to experience the thrill of AHA! in the grand moment of realization of this fact. We bring many actors onto our own personal stage to assist in our mutual awakening process, and to push our buttons until we remember. They will be there when we die to honor our journey and to revel in the joy of that total recall. In this way, we see we are all One, spiritually connected, and separation is an illusion. Once we grasp this, creating our own reality rises to another plane altogether, from getting a parking space to creating constant joy by our conscious application of its principles, mainly that there is no 'right' or 'wrong' in the unconditional love that is each soul's birthright.

~ ~ ~

In our human walk, we see suffering all arou[...]
be in joy. The world and the media seem t[...]
pain, conflict, injustice, and horror. Knowing that,
How do we walk our daily path, remain open, ana [...]
overwhelmed by it all? We have a choice. We can either choose t[...]
on and see the joy and perfection in all that occurs, or we can join the
mainstream and go down the drain of agony, despair, pain,
disappointment and fear. We stand in a flowing stream at a crossroads.
To reach the ocean, we can flow down the sewer or choose to flow
down a lovely river instead. The choice is ours. We can say yes to it all if
we see the perfection in each person as a creator instead of a victim.
Each journey is perfect and offers different opportunities for perception.
At each point, in each moment of time on our journey, we can choose
our perspective, our view and hence the world we experience. But that
crossroads is not just in one place; it is in each experience, every place
in the stream, and in every moment. In each now, we are brought a new
opportunity to choose whether we perceive things from our limited
human perspective or our grander spiritual perspective.

We are perfect, exactly as we are. By this I mean that no one is
broken or needs to be fixed. No matter what circumstance you find
yourself in, there is a reason for it. Once you see what does not serve
you any longer in your world, then as a creator, you can either change
it or change your perspective of it. Based on each small shift, you
create the reality of your next moment.

The Key to Creating Our Reality

We create by *what we think coupled with our emotions. We must then let go of
them AND of the need for a particular outcome.* By letting go, we give our
emotions space to exist and be created. By hanging on, we prevent
them from reaching full creation.

Emotions are the real wave on which we ride through life's journey but most of us have been trained to shut them off and search intellectually for reasons and answers. All emotions are valid by virtue of feeling them. You will continue having feelings of course, but as you apply these principles you will notice they lessen in their intensity and your reactiveness decreases. You will neither have to act upon a feeling nor judge it. You will simply feel it, acknowledge it and allow it. To reach this acceptance that you create your reality through your emotions, start by learning to pay attention to your emotions objectively. You'll have to start *feeling,* and listening to those feelings.

As you can see, this means creating your reality is about an internal process, not an external one. How you deal with thoughts and emotions, all internal, determines how your world appears, what materializes in it, and how you relate to it.

How I Came to Choose Joy

Years ago, as I began this metaphysical journey, I sat in Rajni's class and he said, *"In the midst of any crisis you can choose joy. Joy is always a choice."* At that moment, my life was crashing all around me. The bank had failed taking me with it and now I faced multiple foreclosures on my approximately seven hundred mortgages.

For every foreclosure, I received four notices by mail and four by process servers. I dreaded the doorbell ringing. Every process server in town knew me. When the mailman came, I had to sign for registered mail, which meant more lawsuits. On more than one occasion, the entire two foot long cardboard mail tray was all for me. I had to sign hundreds of receipts to accept these notices, affirming my shame and humiliation. It was so bad that eventually, when selecting an attorney to handle our divorce, we couldn't find one. They were all suing us! Locating one to represent us took eighteen months!

As I heard Raj speak of choosing joy in each moment, I knew that if metaphysics were real, it could be applied everywhere, even out in the real world, and be demonstrated. I absolutely had to know. I decided to apply these words the next time I had to deal with the process servers. I didn't have long to wait. The very next morning, ding-dong, the doorbell rang. I decided to choose joy in that moment and to experience the process server differently. Instead of hiding up against the wall so he couldn't see me through the glass panel, I put on a smile, pumped up my energy, felt joy and opened up the door. I was determined to make this a different experience. It was the postman this time and he had more notices to sign. I said, "My, isn't it a gorgeous day!"

He agreed and added, "Yes, it's my anniversary and we're going to dinner tonight."

On and on he chatted, happily focused on his joy, not my crisis. I was not the center of his world. The embarrassment was all mine. I was astounded. I'd learned to sign my name very quickly. Finished, I closed the door and was still smiling. "This stuff really works!" I gleefully said to myself. Imagine, I had just been notified that I was losing another half million dollars in properties and I was still in joy. WOW! I had found the right path for me. I was on my way and had just taken my first step.

Attorneys Make Me an Offer I Can Refuse

A short time later, I received a call from a prestigious law firm in Seattle. They heard about my situation. Who hadn't? It was front-page news and they wanted to meet with me about recouping my losses. In their impressive conference room, they spoke of a recent successful lawsuit where they had won a multi-million dollar case for a client against a bank for exactly what I had experienced, basically a withdrawn commitment. They said they could guarantee between fifty and one hundred million dollars in damages.

I asked, "How long do you think it would take?"

"About five years," was their reply.

As I thought about it, sitting there in their world of law, I knew it would really take seven or more years and I didn't want to spend those years, day in and day out, proving to myriad people, institutions, and the press that I was a victim. I did not want to become the person I knew I would be if I focused seven years or more of my life proving things I no longer believed, such as that I had not created, albeit unconsciously, this fiasco, since I now believed I had. I truly understood that *what we focus on we get more of.* I was *not* willing to focus on being a victim and proving it. I would rather spend those same years much more productively creating a joyful life and allowing the past to fall away. I wanted joy and knew the money from the lawsuit wouldn't bring it. Time, unclouded with victim mindset, was more precious. I was already confirming that fact every day. I had learned to create joy myself through my own actions and paying attention to my feelings. Although I knew I'd have nothing left, it was an easy choice. By then I knew I was creating my own reality and I knew what I wanted to create and what I didn't.

We are the Source of All Our Feelings

We are the source of all our feelings. We are the source of all the love, hate, anger, and fear that appears in our life. We get stuck in believing that someone else said or did something that made us mad, or made us feel good, or made our day. Actually, they are just reflecting how we unconsciously already feel about ourselves. No one can make us feel anything but everything is a trigger for our feelings. (A "trigger" is a phrase, comment, smirk, body gesture or the absence of what is expected, that ego interprets causing a response in us. There are thousands of triggers for each of us.) But remember, we can choose how to react.

We *can* come from our centered self, that part which remains calm, knowing, balanced emotionally and spiritually, and be present with a feeling, that is, allow ourselves to fully experience any feeling in the very same moment it happens, or we can allow the trigger to find its target and react as usual, feeling angry, jealous, happy, beautiful, or sad. We become reactive if we feel there is a grain of truth in the trigger.

It seems odd to think it is not a good idea to let someone make us feel beautiful. But, think about it. If we are always looking to those outside ourselves to make us feel beautiful, how could we ever feel beautiful if they stopped reinforcing us? What if they moved away, or got angry with us, or died? And what if we became burned or scarred or just older? These are external and superficial reinforcements to self-worth, which continued reliance upon is highly destructive.

It often feels that others are 'making us feel' one way or another, but in truth, no one else is responsible for how we feel. I acknowledge that this seems like a radical view, since all our socialization trains us to feel the opposite: "*You* make me so happy/sad." This stance makes others responsible for us and gives away our power. When we shift from "Why did all this happen to me?" to "How did I create this?" we will shift out of blame and into self-empowerment. We free ourselves from our own fears and limitations. Hiding within ourselves and faking invulnerability with a stiff upper lip is quite different from being truly invulnerable from an authentic position of strength and emotional honesty. The paradox is that our true freedom and invulnerability come from being compassionate, emotionally available and totally vulnerable!

Knowing we each create our own reality is not license to harshly exclaim "That's your problem if you don't like what I did/said." At its heart this is true, but since we are all One in spirit, there is a level of connection in the situation, perhaps even a reflection, blame, fear or guilt. We may wish to distance ourselves from our empathic feeling of the other's pain. Such blatant behavior misuses this knowledge and abuses others with it. Such ancient wisdom is really meant to permit compassion, allowance, connection and understanding and to remind us we are in the act of creating and can choose again to create differently. Feel the fear, feel the compassion and allow it all.

Most people are afraid of their own power. Owning that we are the creators of our reality is truly empowering. Most people are unaware they have any power at all and would prefer to let others make all the decisions because there would be someone to blame if need be. If we stood in our own power, there would be no one else to blame and we would have to shift our whole perspective on life. We could no longer say, "Life just happens, I am only an observer."

How Can We Be the Source of All Our Feelings?

The following story illustrates how we are the authors of our own feelings. Imagine you are sitting at a table having a conversation with a friend and you are suddenly kicked in the shins. You react first with pain, "Ow!" Then anger, "Why did you do that?" Then judgment, "What's wrong with you?" Then with self-judgment and fear, "What's wrong with me that you would do such a thing?" Then you look under the table and see a Great Dane puppy, asleep and kicking at something in a dream. Your anger dissipates in laughter, self-worth is back intact, soreness diminishes. No more guilt and blame, no more fear or judgment, no more pain.

All your feelings were real by virtue of the fact that they existed. You and you alone were the author of them. No one else caused them. That kick was a trigger and you took the ride alone. There is always a trigger and we always choose whether to **act** from the center of our being, where we know who we are, or to **react** out of imbalance, victimhood, and fear.

Learn To Ask Why

We may respond with "Ow!" but if we would then ask ourselves, "Why did I create this?" We would not look to guilt or blame because we would know it no longer serves us to march down that path if we intend to create joy.

By asking, "Why did I create this?" we own the fact that we are creators of our experience. Not as victims, but as true creators. Once we know how we create, we can apply that knowledge in a different way to create what we prefer in our lives. Thus we empower ourselves, knowing we are true creators in concert with our higher selves and in alignment with our divine connection.

Overcoming Resistance

We defiantly resist the idea that we create our reality. It gives us a supposed sense of security to believe that some higher power, some other person or some unseen force, is pulling our strings and that 'they' are in charge, perhaps parents, government, mate or boss. Most times, the results of our actions can be seen so quickly that we can easily identify the prime force in our creation. For example, when we walk on ice and slip and fall, we realize we weren't taking care on a precarious surface. (Of course, most of the time, we want to blame whoever should have cleared the sidewalk.)

The cause-and-effect of walking carelessly on ice and falling down is obvious, but it is less obvious to see ourselves as creators when effects manifest long after the cause, such as with illness. We don't see that our deep-set fears about moving forward in life created our sprained ankle, or that feeling burdened by the problems we 'shoulder' actually created our stiff shoulders. We don't see the burn we just got on our hand was from our fearful belief that what we are handling is way too 'hot' for us.

As we proceed to monitor our experiences consciously, we will become more and more adept at choosing, changing and creating a better one, both in long and short term events.

Matt Triggers a Feeling Storm

This story is an example of how we take emotional journeys all by ourselves and just how responsible we are for our own feelings. It happened as I was learning how I created my own reality.

After my neighbor, Matt, told me he was leaving on vacation for two weeks, I discovered his car in my parking space, a perfect trigger. It was a wet winter and my space was covered, his wasn't. I was angry. I couldn't understand why he had done this. It didn't seem like him. For several days, I considered having his car towed but didn't.

Then I personalized his conduct as retaliation for something I'd said to him that had embarrassed him. I felt his embarrassment and subsequent hasty departure after our conversation were judgments of my behavior. Then I began to consider alternative explanations. Maybe a friend drove him to the airport and parked the car in the wrong space. Or maybe Matt had been drunk or in a hurry. I went back and forth but mostly I felt put down, inferior, unacknowledged, excluded, insulted even though I knew I was certainly making a mountain out of a molehill. I couldn't help myself.

When Matt came home, I began to get angry all over again by replaying my injured party tape. Suddenly I realized I was only waiting to hear his reason so I could justify all my feelings. It dawned on me that I'd caused them, was responsible for them all. Even when I learn the reason, I thought, I will still be responsible for what I'd felt.

So there I sat, to catch Matt as he emerged from his apartment but still wondered where my asking "Why?" would get me. To feel satisfied that I wasn't slighted? Justification for my anger? It hadn't rained while he was gone, so I hadn't really been inconvenienced. Then I remembered I had a frozen lock because of exposure in his space, and became angry again.

I finally decided I'd created the whole episode for the purpose of seeing that *I*, not Matt, or anyone else, had created all my feelings. He may have been the trigger, but I was the puppet master jerking my own strings.

Eventually, curiosity got the best of me and I did ask. "My friend took me to the airport, drove the car back and parked it in the wrong space," he said. No apology came. Now I had the opportunity of feeling hurt all over again but I stopped. I'd learned about creating my own "feeling storm," and simply decided not to go there this time. I believe I manifested this non-apology as another opportunity to choose how I would react. It was my first exam and I'd passed. I did not get back on the emotional roller coaster. I felt emotionally powerful for the first time and I've had many such experiences since.

This story demonstrates the teaching that in any situation we have control over the acknowledgment of our feelings and our choice of how or when to react to them. In the heat of any turmoil, the object is not to fix the problem, get rid of it or do war on it. The object is to change our perceptions about it. We are totally in charge of how we respond to our environment. Eventually, as we begin to act from the center of our being in the midst of crisis, we will have successfully moved beyond the self-testing of our higher selves. We will no longer need to create more experiences that bring us face-to-face with the same emotional hurdles. In other words, when we learn how to stop reacting from old fear-based patterns of unlovability, lack of self-worth, lack of control, lack of sufficiency and separation fears, we will have broken the pattern of our subconscious and avoided perpetuating the same hurdles.

In real world results, our lives will flow more smoothly. We won't be the ones stuck on the freeway in a traffic jam. We won't be the ones whose package is lost in the mail. We won't be the ones who get behind the chatty customer in the check out stand when we're in a hurry. These things will no longer occur in our lives because our focus will have shifted. We will be flowing our energy in ease instead of resistance. Our lives will be easier. When we're in the flow of life's events instead of constantly fighting an uphill battle, we do not get caught in the same trap as does the angry, upset, frustrated, fearful person.

These are baby steps we need when we first begin to consciously monitor our thoughts, words and actions. Over time, many successful little experiences will lead us to creating a world that flows and is tension-free. Resistance creates more resistance; flow creates more flow.

"I Love You"

Three women once sat in my office in a spiritual group counseling session. These are often intense and deeply emotional experiences. I said to them from the bottom of my heart "I love you." Each one heard and interpreted that same statement through the veils of their own fears. Enraptured, one said, "That is the most loving thing I have ever felt." The second looked blank at the others and said, "What does she mean?" The third smirked in disgust and said, "She's gay."

Each of us responds to stimuli from our own center. If that center is fear-based, we are playing a victim role. If it's love-based, then we truly hear with our hearts and in the vibration of love. This is being "centered in self." It is always a loving space. Which of the three would you be? If a wonderful expression such as "I love you" can generate such misinterpretations, how much more miscommunication might occur in everyday comments and normal conversations?

We cannot control how others interpret what we say. At best, we can only offer unconditional love.

Next, we will look at how we may view any situation to make sense of it and interpret it from our newfound perspective.

Chapter 3

The Law of Triadic Creation

The Law of Triadic Creation is an arrangement of two triangles, one of Love positioned above one of Fear, each point labeled with a role that can be played. These triangles reflect clearly and simply what is happening in any situation, thereby offering a choice to shift from FEAR to LOVE.

I learned this technique from Rajni, who used it again and again to demonstrate and clarify how situations were either love- or fear-based.

We create our lives moment to moment. The greatest duality is whether we create out of Love or out of Fear. All our interactions and endeavors, great or small, are contained in these two triangles. All our experiences fall into some part of these triads and every circumstance can be interpreted through one or the other.

When we create out of Love, we act simultaneously as Giver to Self, Receiver of what we gave, and Accepter of what was given and received.

When we create from Fear, we are simultaneously Victim, Persecutor, and Rescuer. In either triangle, we can play one or all of the roles.

The triads consist of two triangles labeled to show the bi-directional energy flow and the roles we play in a situation. We can see in an instant what the dynamics really are and make our choices accordingly.

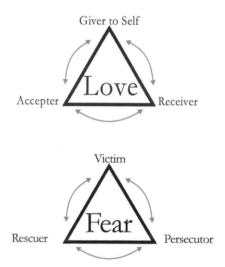

Note that the Love Triangle, the higher vibration of the two, sits above the Fear Triangle.

In the Love triangle, we operate from our highest Self, which is allowing, non-judgmental, nurturing, centered and loving. In the Fear triangle, where all aspects focus on things outside of us, and appear to have control over our lives, we operate from a limited, fearful Self who needs protection and is ever watchful.

Understanding and using Triadic Creation, you can learn to create the love-based reality that will liberate you from a world of victimhood and fear. How is this done? When you identify the fears in a situation, either simply be aware or help to allay them. If you see fear of lack of control, then give the fearful person control in some situation; fear of lack, remind them that the universe is abundant; fear of separation, include them; fear of unlovability, love them; fear of lack of self-worth, show them their value. (More on these fears in Chapter 5.) This is real power, to reveal and honor a person's innate value and essence.

Its great values as a working tool for positive life changes are that it:

- Is presented as a simple graphic, not a set of rules.
- Is fast and you can apply it while still in the middle of the conversation or situation.
- Offers an instantaneous way to re-see a situation so you avoid programmed reactions and can make choices for the reality you want now.
- Forces you to step back from the event, so you escape being sucked into the drama and losing yourself in emotion.
- Allows you to break complicated scenarios into manageable parts and look at them one by one (the triad behind the triad behind the triad—because of that, and because of that, and because of that, this happened …
- Can be applied to all situations without exception.
- Shows you in what manner you can allay others' fears.

Our world is one of dualities-hot and cold, up and down, left and right. We learn about our world by experiencing such pairs of opposites. We know cold because we experience its opposite, hot. We can then choose consciously between opposites from an informed perspective.

We don't have to burn ourselves to understand the implications of too hot. We also do not need to learn through suffering, pain, drama or trauma, although we can. It's always an option. Extremes are unnecessary, unless we think they are. We direct our own lives. We are in conscious command.

You can see that the Love triad is Giving/Receiving/Accepting and the Fear triad is Victim/Persecutor/Rescuer. Subsequent discussions in the following chapters will add to your understanding of these relationships.

First, the LOVE Triad, the upper triangle:

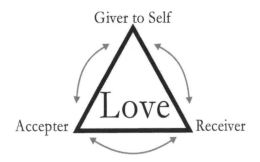

- *Giver to Self* at the apex is you, recognizing that whatever you give to yourself you are giving to all because all are One. This self is your higher Self, one who is calm, knowing and spiritually connected. When you give to others, you are always also Giving to Self.
- *Receiver* means One who receives what is given, whether from self or others.
- *Accepter* means One who is able to physically, emotionally and mentally accept what has been received, aligning with what is received *without judgment*, **knowing** receiving is giving and giving is receiving. The essence of each is contained within the other. True acceptance is accomplished as each of us understands we all are One, inextricably connected by divine inheritance.

Here are some typical relationships shown in Love Triads below:
1. A loving mother and her baby,
2. A cheerful cook preparing a meal for diners,
3. A superb teacher with her students.

Mother and Baby

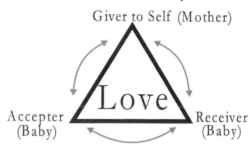

Cook and Diners

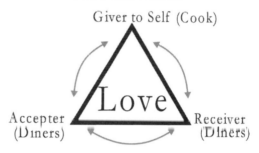

Teacher and Students

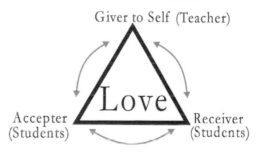

In the simplified triads above, each actor plays all three roles when all are enjoying the experience.

Second, The FEAR Triad, the Lower Triangle:

This is easier to grasp because unfortunately, we seem much more familiar with it!

- **Victim**, at the apex, is one who perceives him/herself as separate, powerless, unworthy, inadequate, wrong, and controlled by others, unknown whim, luck or predestined fate.

- **Persecutor** means one who is viewed as a victim maker, in control, arbitrary, powerful, separate and judgmental.

- **Rescuer** means one who acts as a savior in relationship to 'Others'

In each of these three roles, the individual has forgotten his or her Oneness with others.

Here is an example of how this works. Think of a time when you were shopping and found that exquisite cashmere, hand-detailed sweater, exactly what you've always wanted, even though it was *really* expensive. It looked and felt wonderful, fit perfectly and you bought it! You're in the Love Triangle (*Giver*). You wore it home feeling like a million dollars (*Receiver*). But the next morning you wake up and upon seeing it, felt sick (Non-*Accepter*). You flip immediately into the Fear Triangle. "How could I have spent that much?" (*Victim*) you ask yourself in the bathroom mirror. You scolded yourself, repeating the price over and over, making your guilt worse (*Persecutor*). You felt you must return it (*Rescuer*). Congratulations. You are playing all three Fear roles!

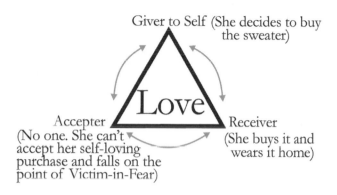

Giver to Self (She decides to buy the sweater)

Accepter (No one. She can't accept her self-loving purchase and falls on the point of Victim-in-Fear)

Love

Receiver (She buys it and wears it home)

Victim (Of her own joy and self-love)

Rescuer (She returns the sweater)

Fear

Persecutor (By herself for her extravagance)

Our shopper was doing beautifully until the next morning when her inability to Accept caused her to impale herself on the Victim point of the lower Fear triangle. Her self-worth and money issues made her incapable of Receiving from herself.

Time and again, in any situation, we can use the Law of Triadic Creation to figure out what is really going on and what roles we are playing. I have yet to find a single circumstance that the two triangles do not encompass. Using this tool, we can view any circumstance or relationship from a new and higher perspective. Doing so will change you. It will change your outlook, your health, your self-worth, your abundance, and your relationships. Everything shifts to a higher plane when you use your new perspective to see through judgment, hate, anger, and any other non-loving experiences. Remember, any action, feeling or experience that is non-loving is fear-based.

Let's look at the same three Love triad examples from page 21 when they are not loving.

Mother frustrated by baby's constant needs

Victim 1) Mother feeling overwhelmed
2) Baby when mother
withholds love

Rescuer
1) Mother as she stops
withholding love
2) Some third person, mate
caregiver, nurse, grandparent

Persecutor
1) Mother - towards baby
2) Baby - as perceived by
mother

Cook hates her job

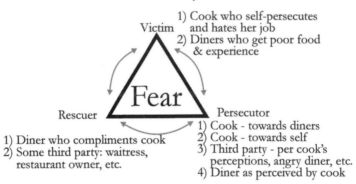

1) Cook who self-persecutes
Victim   and hates her job
2) Diners who get poor food
& experience

Rescuer
1) Diner who compliments cook
2) Some third party: waitress,
restaurant owner, etc.

Persecutor
1) Cook - towards diners
2) Cook - towards self
3) Third party - per cook's
perceptions, angry diner, etc.
4) Diner as perceived by cook

Teacher resents students

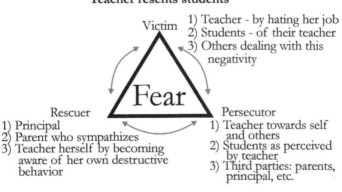

Victim 1) Teacher - by hating her job
2) Students - of their teacher
3) Others dealing with this
negativity

Rescuer
1) Principal
2) Parent who sympathizes
3) Teacher herself by becoming
aware of her own destructive
behavior

Persecutor
1) Teacher towards self
and others
2) Students as perceived
by teacher
3) Third parties: parents,
principal, etc.

Just from these few examples you can immediately see how we create our own reality—the same people in different roles at different times. Here are a few more to give you both sides of similar situations:

- Neighbor wins the Lotto and begins having great fun with the money. Love Triangle.
- You win the Lotto but fear all your relatives hitting you up for money. Fear Triangle.
- You love your job and your boss gives you a raise. Love Triangle.
- You wake up every morning hating the thought of going to work and today you get laid off. Fear Triangle.
- You get laid off, seeing it as an opportunity to start your own business. Love Triangle.

- The neighbor's cat has kittens. The kids see the miracle of life. All are healthy. Love Triangle.
- Those same cats grow up, kill the local squirrels, use your flowerbeds as a toilet and sharpen their claws on your wooden hot tub and you get upset. Fear Triangle.

- Driving home someone cuts you off in traffic and you get angry. Fear Triangle.
- When cut off while driving, you take it as a sign to pay more careful attention to driving, avoiding rear-ending another vehicle. Love Triangle.

- The woman in front of you in the checkout line has 340 coupons. Delayed, you get frustrated. Fear Triangle.
- Same checkout line delay but you begin a conversation with another person in line and discover it's your old high school chum. Love Triangle.

~ ~ ~

Exercise. Now you try. List 5 situations. Draw and label the triads to see how this works. Practice seeing how interactions appear and the choices becoming available that you didn't know were there.

You'll find many other examples in this book as they come up in the categories of money, relationships, authority figures, the body and crisis. Think how you would have reacted in the past. Create your reality anew with the triads, seeing how different life would be if you chose to create out of Love.

The next two chapters will examine Love and Fear more closely.

Chapter 4

The Nature of Love

Love has no agenda. Love has no goal. Love has no ego attachment. Love has no underlying purpose for being. Love is timeless, expanding all time into this now. Love is totally free and without limitation. Love is without conditions of any sort. Love is our natural state of being.

When we are in love, the very beginning of that "Oh so exceptional" relationship with Mr. or Ms. Perfect, it doesn't matter where we are or what we are doing. Nothing spoils it. We go out to eat and the atmosphere is dank and dingy. It doesn't matter. We're in love. They're out of the salmon we've ordered. No big deal. We're in love. We get caught in the rain. No problem. We're with that special someone and it doesn't matter. In fact, we laugh about it all. Love does that. It raises our vibrations. It gives us rose-colored glasses. It lifts us up to a higher perspective. It comes from within and is reflected all around us. This is the Love Triad.

Happy, joy-filled people just stand out. Their joy cup is so full that it overflows, falling on everyone and everything around them. It has a magnetic quality that attracts others, drawing them to it like warm sun on a winter morning. Like the sun, it has no need to shine, but it cannot do otherwise. That is what love is and what it does. Love is a state of being that spills over the boundaries of the Self, naturally, wholesomely, joyfully. The vibration of Love and its sister emotion, Joy, are the highest examples of life that we can be.

Love means:
1. We have no goal, no need for any particular outcome, no hanging on to expectations. Many self help books discuss goal setting, which is the opposite of what love is. Goal-setting causes you to live in the future, to base self worth on achievement of objectives and puts values outside of oneself. This is for people who think that once they achieve something they will be lovable. More often than not, we fall short of those goals and feel disappointed, unworthy and unhappy. They simply become another tool for self-abuse.
2. We are not ego-based (exclusionary of others). The ego is in balance since its worth is not based on any expectation of outcome. The ego acknowledges it and all others are One. It simply IS.
3. We are unconditional. Freed from hanging on to an expected outcome, we allow it ALL.
4. We are unlimited. Our thoughts and actions no longer include can't, shouldn't, only and never. Freed from limitation, we experience being much more, and we allow ourselves to experience whatever happens.
5. We are judgment free. We remain in the free flow of allowance so that the unseen reveals itself, including the unseen self.

Judgment is the quality of defining a thing in relationship to another as better, bigger, uglier, tastier. Love exists in the world of the absolute, (Oneness, Isness, free of duality). It allows, encompasses and accepts all *as it is* without any such need for comparison as exists in the world of duality. Love transcends duality.

6. We are open to access and align with higher wisdom, that part of us that remains connected to God.

7. We cannot be victims.

8. We remain in the Now, staying focused on the present moment.

Loving Ourselves as We Love Others

The Golden Rule teaches us to love one another *as we love ourselves*. This does not mean that we love ourselves *less than* we love others; nor does it mean that we love ourselves *more than* others. We do not have to be first nor put ourselves last. We don't have to be persecutors or rescuers. It's not about being average. It's about putting ourselves on an equal footing with others. We have opportunities to see this a hundred times a day in small, seemingly insignificant ways. Life changes are mostly achieved by remaining focused and aware in small everyday events rather than in a blazing series of great cosmic awakenings.

For example, suppose you're barbecuing hamburgers for eight, all old friends. You burn one of the burgers. Most people as victims have been taught to quietly eat the mistake themselves. *I am the host, I must serve my guests the best I can offer. My self-worth is directly connected to how well I make them feel comfortable and liked. In turn, I hope that they will reward me with acceptance, compliments and approval because without it, I am not good enough. It was stupid to burn the burger. It's better to hide my blunder. Of course I'll take the burnt burger as I am guilty and I'll certainly not mention it to anyone. I can suffer through it easily knowing I've made my friends happy.*

Great. So let's look at all these stunning belief systems. I am less than everyone else but should appear perfect at all times. Any mistake, no matter how slight, is a reflection of my stupidity and lack of worth, in fact, of being 'bad'. All mistakes must be hidden. The charade must go on. I don't deserve anything better than my worst effort. I am a Victim of my own efforts and I must Rescue myself lest I be embarrassed and Persecuted by my guests, my mate or others.

1) Me, who burned the
   hamburgers, worthless me
2) Guests, if I served them
   burned hamburgers

Victim

Fear

Rescuer

1) Me, by hiding my flaw,
   punishing self by eating
   the burnt one
2) Someone else who takes
   the burnt one

Persecutor

1) Me. I am a bad cook & person.
   I need their love to be okay.
2) Guests, if I serve burnt
   hamburgers

How might you handle this situation if you operate out of the Love triad? You would love yourself and know you are a perfect human, you are a creator, everything happens for a reason and there are no accidents? You are equal to all others, who are responsible for their own feelings and you cannot "make" them happy, sad or angry. They do that themselves. If you really knew all this, you would take the burnt hamburger only one out of every eight times. You might then hold up the burnt burger on a fork and with a laugh announce, "I burned one. It's not my turn. Who wants it?"

Someone may say they prefer the burnt one and actually mean it! (If your friends have read this book, they may say, "I don't like burnt ones and it's not my turn either!")

More likely, the Rescuer with the greatest issues about self-worth, feeling less than, making others happy, keeping the peace, and sacrifice will immediately offer with something like, "Oh I just love burnt ones. I actually prefer them." But deep inside, they can't stand them.

If you only take the burnt burger one out of eight times, then you have put yourself on an equal footing of love with all other guests. In fact, you have acknowledged that you and they are One. You are not responsible for their feelings. You have self-empowered guests. You support their ability to choose for themselves and to love themselves enough to say "yes" or "no," evenly. This is loving yourself **as** another— not less than, not more than.

This may appear a trivial example, but think of your life and how many times a day you give yourself away in small pieces and tiny, seemingly inconsequential actions of self-sacrifice like this one. You do this because you think you should, but you don't really want to and you don't yet know how to stop the process and comfortably say "No."

Little by little, we erase parts of ourselves and our desires until we virtually disappear. Only then does it become so painful we finally choose ourselves. By that time, those choices can be radical —big departures from the usual 'you'. For example, suppose you're at a friend's house. It's hot and you're really thirsty but, when offered a glass of water, you say, "Oh, just a small glass." Asked if you want ice, "Oh don't go to any trouble."

Only when you stop meeting situations in the role of victim or persecutor and love yourself enough will you give yourself permission to simply ask for what you want. This is but a small scenario, but stand in your own power and ask for the tall, delicious glass of ice water you really want. Your host or hostess will love pleasing you. Should they be tempted to think they are rescuing you as victims, your joyful self-empowered attitude will show them you believe yourself as entitled to the drink as they would be in your home!

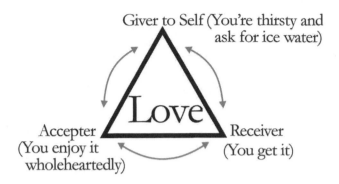

Unconditional Love

Love without conditions means just that-no conditions, no strings, no shoulds, no requirements, no expectations, no needs, no goals and a willingness to let go. Take gift giving. Getting hurt feelings if we are not 'properly' thanked for a gift we've given is conditional love. We placed the condition that the Receiver must show appropriate appreciation, even if only a "Thank you." If our desired response isn't forthcoming, we resent it and end up becoming a victim of giving a gift! Sometimes we expect to receive a gift in return and are highly insulted when we don't—only because we put a string or condition on our giving. Suppose you bought an expensive pair of jogging shoes. After a day or so, you realize they don't fit that well, but instead of taking them back, decide to give them to the family with seven children across the street. You know they don't have much and the shoes would certainly fit one of them. So you feel really good about yourself, you giver you. A week later, they have a garage sale and you find your jogging shoes for sale at a high price. How do you feel? Used, backstabbed, unappreciated? How dare they make money off your gift! Don't they know how to receive? If this is how you feel, then you had strings attached to your gift. You still considered them your shoes. You didn't let go and now you've hurt yourself.

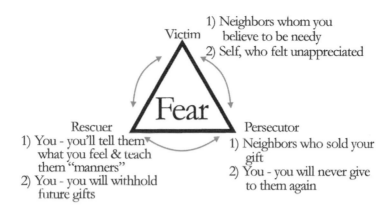

In relationships for instance, because we often attach so many strings to our love for others—and they to theirs for us—it becomes almost impossible to be authentic and open. We often give our love only if the other person performs according to our needs or wishes, such as loving us in return *in the way we want to be loved*. If they don't, they must pay! How quickly we switch from victim to persecutor. To meet the conditional requirements of such love, both parties become observers, looking for the signals that indicate how we should respond in order to be loved. Conditional love is highly destructive to honesty, vulnerability and emotional availability.

A real gift is freely given. The receiver doesn't even have to accept it, much less appreciate it or even use it as you intended. A real gift ends with the giving, or else it is conditional. How often we do this daily in our relationships: I'll do this for you, but you better do such and such in return. There are unspoken words, but a demand is made just the same, and all too often we keep score. But remember, this is just one choice. After all, how would you seek thanks from a bird who's wing you fixed? What expectations would you have? Would you feel approval or disapproval based on whether it chirruped or communicated some form of appreciation?

~ ~ ~

A good friend, Frances, seemed to understand non-attachment to gifts. She received many, especially from her mother. When she decided to relocate, she sold most of her belongings, including those given to her by her mother. When her mother learned of this, she was shocked and incensed. She became angry and hateful towards the 'ungrateful' child. She had no understanding of gift giving.

It happened that Frances had given me a dish that I loved. Ten years later, my neighbor, Velda, fell in love with it and since I was no longer so attached to it I offered it to her as a gift. She insisted on paying something and gave me $50.

In a later conversation with Frances, I told her of my successful experience with detachment, in which art she already excelled. I was surprised, therefore, when Frances got mad, really mad. She was furious that I had not just given away, but actually sold, her gift. I was shocked and tried to explain I hadn't sold it, merely accommodated the recipient's demand to pay. I wondered what happened to all that detachment and understanding regarding gifts? Frances was still measuring her value by how others regarded gifts she gave—extensions of herself— but she felt free to dispose of gifts she received from others—extensions of them. This double standard was a new twist for me on conditional love. This is obviously the Fear Triad.

Moving from fear-based creation to love-based creation requires us to begin looking at how we seek reward, acknowledgement, inclusion, and acceptance from others. When we believe these things originate outside of us, we continue to seek them by manipulating others through our behavior. Once we are consciously aware that we are already the source of all these things, we can then stop seeking them from others, letting go of our fears.

Let's examine fear more closely.

Chapter 5

The Nature of Fear

Fear is anything that is not loving. Fear is limited. Fear is constricting. Fear is conditional. Fear is living in the past or the future, but not in the now. Fear has an agenda. Fear is fixated on outcome. Fear is a learned state of being. It is not our natural state.

The Five Main Fears are:

- **Fear of Unlovability**
- **Fear of Lack of self-worth**
- **Fear of Lack**
- **Fear of Lack of control**
- **Fear of Separation.**

One or more of these fears is in play whenever we are involved with or behaving as a Rescuer, a Persecutor, or a Victim—the roles in the lower triangle. All of them can be present at once, for instance, in a divorce court. We find fear of unlovability and lack of self-worth when we think that if we'd been lovable or good enough in the first place, we wouldn't be getting divorced, and an inner voice whispers over and over, "You aren't lovable. No one else will put up with you. Something's wrong with you. You're not good enough."

Lack of control is present in not knowing how the court will decide; and we find separation in the divorce itself. Fear of lack of course exists in the unsure division of assets.

In other words, we now believe that it is our actions that make us lovable. All our self-worth is tied up in what we **do**, not who we **are**. We can't see that we will ever be chosen and loved by anyone else. Society has taught that we are now undesirable in new ways: age, debts and children, labeled by divorce. We equate our lovability with these external realities. We give up. We can't fool anyone. We believe no one is going to love us, so why bother. And that scenario is exactly what we will create.

Fear, as used in this book, is not fear of spiders or walking under ladders, but is about these subconscious, entrenched teachings that we unknowingly let create our reality usually because this serves us in some way — there's a payoff, usually emotional. We get to feel alive, nurtured, included, important or desired. These feelings can all be traced to one or more of these five fears.

Fear of Unlovability

Fear of being unlovable is the single most destructive fear in all the universes, a seething pit of hatred, jealousy, greed, disease, self-destruction, anger, suicide, murder and addiction. We can trace every dysfunction, personal or social, to this fear. "I am not lovable" or "No one loves me" is a feeling learned while still in diapers.

Why Do We Feel Unlovable?

Unlovable means I don't feel good enough to receive love from others in the way in which I expect it and need it. Its unhappy root lies in the belief that feelings come from outside of us, that we are not their source. We usually learn this behavior as children. All families are dysfunctional. It's just the degree of dysfunction that determines the impact on each family member. We may not love a person's behavior, but can still love the person. In other words, we can say "No" to their conduct, and still say "Yes" to the person. This distinction, however, is not apparent to an infant or to a child being chastised, nor for that matter, to an adult feeling shamed.

For example, a young boy kicks someone. "Go to your room until you learn how to behave decently," he is scolded. He feels rejected and isolated. He has failed to meet the expectations of one of the perceived sources of love in his life. He cannot yet separate that it was his action that was unlovable, not him. He also received nonverbal input from the hostile posture of an authority figure bent over him, from the raised pitch of the voice, from the words spoken, from the feelings or 'vibes' of everyone present sending hostility, withdrawal and anger, disgust and shame towards him. All this he experiences, feels and internalizes in his memory and subconscious emotions. Thus is he shaped to conform to society's expectations. The message received is, "They will not love me. I am not lovable if I don't obey, if I don't meet others' expectations, if I'm not good enough". The result being that "I can't live without 'their' love" is deeply internalized from birth. That's how conditional love becomes well entrenched.

With such guidelines, children easily learn that they can never be lovable, because they will never know or meet all the expectations. They are taught they are forever imperfect. Step-by-step, they are taught that they are not lovable under certain circumstances, and the list is legion in number.

This is reinforced as young adults begin dating in a series of tests to see if and how much they are lovable. Thus begins a quest to get someone else to fill up our cup of love. Each of us is a whole, complete being, an expression of God's love, perfect. Most of us need reassurance we are lovable and we seek it from someone else. We walk around, so to speak, with a partially filled cup of love, looking for a mate willing to pour some of theirs into our cup, and vice versa, so we can feel loved. Much of this "love bartering" calls for manipulation, victimhood conduct, guilt, control, shame, should's and ought to's, religious and social obligations and cultural requirements. In other words, the dating game. All of it is a seeking to find out just how lovable we might be.

Reversing Our Unlovability

How do we stop self-loathing? By choosing to focus on the fact that love is not something external to the Self. The source of love is within. We are Love by our very nature. When we focus on that love within, we become the experience of love. We actually create a world around us filled with love, reflecting who we have chosen to be.

Sylvia came for counseling. She had been an executive in a high profile corporation. When her company merged, her job was eliminated. She no longer felt valuable. Her self-worth had been determined by her ability to bring in a large income, by her decision-making and the impact the results had on her clients. Sylvia could not see that she had any worth based on who she was. It was all a case of what she did. She fell into a deep depression, her highly creative and intelligent mind getting in the way of seeing worth in herself just by virtue of her existence. Sylvia was able to go through her depression and find her true worth on the other side.

"As within, so without" is an ancient alchemical teaching, as old as thought. It means that as you perceive yourself to be, it will be so reflected in your world. As you think, so you are. What you are, you create. The emotional state you are in is the source of what your world reflects. Choose to be the expression of love by staying focused on loving thoughts and feelings from memories and experiences, and you will find that your world will change, as if by magic. And it is magic to see reality through new eyes. This is not about being loved or loving someone else. This is about being love itself, about reflecting the radiance of love. Pregnancy causes this state naturally. Pregnant women glow. They are not actively pushing out a glow. It is a vibration, a visible aura radiating from within. It is a reflection of the state of being they are in. It is in this way that we experience the state of *being love.* The same holds true for lovers whose loving vibration is almost tangible from the moment they enter a room.

Allow the love to fill you. Recall every memory that was a loving experience. Dwell on them. Reconnect with the feeling of those experiences. Feel those feelings again. You will radiate love. It is impossible not to. It is your natural state of being, only now you have turned it on consciously.

Look at the workplace on Monday morning. Have you ever come in talking about the wonderful weekend you just had? You had a romantic evening, received a dozen roses, won at bingo or purchased a new car and you want to share it. But your co-workers are all mumbling about how they didn't get enough sleep, had to pay bills, didn't have enough money, how their mates mistreated them on Saturday or their abusive relative humiliated them once again.

Do you have the courage to turn the tide of complaints? Does your lovability quotient depend on their opinion of you? When you can internalize this feature, and turn on your love from within, you will have resolved this issue. When you come from a center of self-love, your presence alone will be sufficient to shift a situation like the Monday morning workplace. The energy you carry will be all that is necessary; you won't have to do anything. You will be radiating love.

Fear of Lack of Self-worth

Often we don't think we're good enough to get that promotion or have the car we want. My parents once rejected a free house to live in because it was too good for them. They said they would feel uncomfortable. They had an image of themselves as not worthy of quality surroundings and it was too good for them. They were actually in fear of having something that surpassed their level of self-worth.

When people exceed their self-worth in business, it's like a rubber band. It stretches as they build the company. Then all the hard work pays off and it's successful beyond their "wildest dreams." How many times have we heard that? The success truly was in the realm of dreams and couldn't remain real. We can survive beyond our perceptions of self-worth for just so long; then the rubber band snaps and the business falters, then fails completely unless the entrepreneurs' self-worth grows with their company. It snaps back to their self-worth comfort zone, their safe and predictable self-image. This is not ego. It is the subconscious mind's perception of personal value, the limits of potential. *No matter what the intellect is avowing, the operating system called the emotional self is really in control.*

That worth is determined from input gained since infancy. If a child's potential is validated, if there is constant encouragement and positive reinforcement, then the self-worth says, "Yes, I can have it all." As the ad says, "I'm worth it." But how many times do we go to the grocery store and say "No" to buying an item we really want because it's too expensive, fattening, elitist, special or unususal? We don't see ourselves in those terms, so we don't buy those items.

Self-worth issues are often apparent when receiving gifts. Think of when you gave a gift to your mother, for instance. My friend Patricia's mother always used to say, "You shouldn't have done this. How much did you spend? We'll take it back. Where did you get it? Did you keep the receipt? I don't need something this expensive. You save your hard earned money." Yes, there were many times when Pat's mother was protecting her from overspending but, once she could well afford it, that was no longer the case. Patricia began to realize that it wasn't about her mother protecting her, but it was her mother's inability to receive. She was saving face. She couldn't accept nice things because she didn't feel worthy.

How many people do we hear about who win the state lottery and are bankrupt within five years. The sudden receipt of a huge amount of money rips them out of their comfort zone and completely outstrips their self-image's ability to possess it. They squander it in order to return to their zone of safety.

Many religions even teach that we aren't worthy of God's love unless we conform to their particular set of interpretations and requirements. To coerce compliance, they say God made these requirements and rules. Others are the subsequent interpreted man-made rules of the religion. Obviously from their perspective God didn't do a complete job.

Considering that God is an unconditionally loving being, there is no need to earn worthiness. Our very existence is proof of our worthiness. We are already the inheritor of God's love. We don't have to do or be anything. We already are a reflection of that perfect love. Worthiness requirements are the result of man-made rules that allow religions and organizations to control us and our behavior. Fearful interpretations of love, which include conditions and judgment, dis-empower the individual and are the real basis of fear of lack of self-worth. Being love based by our very nature, an individual will seek the highest spiritual path, unless it is trained or beaten out of him. Many well-intentioned teachers have physically, emotionally and psychologically damaged their students. So too do many religions that once were divinely inspired.

Exercise to Increase Self-Worth

Make a list of what you feel are all your positive qualities. Fill in the blank: "I am beautiful or handsome because _____." I am lovable because _____."

Becky's Exam

Becky took the final exam for her physiology class. She had obtained a copy of last year's exam and studied it diligently. She spent two days studying round the clock and even slept at the college. She was a high-energy overachiever, putting great focus into everything she did. Her classmates and friends knew she was a hard worker with high ethical standards. The day of the exam arrived. She was supremely prepared and proud of the intensity of her studying. The exam was the duplicate of last year's and she was shocked. She got an A, as did her entire study group and other study groups who had studied with that exam. The professor was amazed there were so many A's. Becky wanted to spill the beans and tell him but her classmates said no. Becky felt sorry for the students who had flunked the exam, feeling they hadn't had the extra benefit she felt she'd had by studying the previous year's exam.

She asked my opinion. It was clear she was feeling the need to rescue the other students, but why? Which of the five fears was at work? Remember, she prides herself in committing to her studies and all the hard work she put in to it. She didn't get acknowledged for all that work. Her issue was lack of self-worth. She was looking outside herself to be validated for all her efforts in order to acknowledge her self-worth. Realizing this changed her whole perspective. It didn't eliminate the need for her self-worth, but it did let her see what was really going on and what her real motivations were. She realized that in aspects of her own worthiness and her need to rescue, she was operating out of the Fear Triad.

In addition to her self-worth issues, I reminded her that she was forgetting that those students who got low scores were each creators of their own realities also. She was in essence saying, "I know how you should do your life better than you. You are broken but I know how to fix you." They were all aware of the study groups but had made different choices. That's just the point. We are all allowed to make our own choices. For us, they are the best choices, because we are all on individual paths.

We don't always know the ultimate outcome of individual creations until later. We can speculate though. Perhaps those students who did not do well in the class halted their life direction and didn't become a nurse or doctor and didn't give the wrong medication to a patient ten years later, thus saving a life. Or perhaps the student changed careers and became a car mechanic and fixed the brakes on a vehicle that prevented a fatal accident.

Our best path is to allow for all possible outcomes and remain judgment-free. We can stay in awareness and trust that whatever is happening in any situation is in the highest and best interests of those involved, whether or not we ever see the final outcome. Don't stop the flow of events. Remove the judgment. Allow.

Once she got past the need to rescue the other students, Becky then focused on the professor. "Shouldn't I tell him so he can change the exam next year?" she asked.

"Sounds like you've hit the core issue now," I replied. "You want your validation directly from the one person from whom it would be the most valuable. When you tell him of the 'problem,' then he will know how much you studied and hopefully will acknowledge it for you. It's still a self worth issue." Becky decided not to tell the professor.

Teachers Can Limit or Open a Mind

Likewise, the best **life** teachers understand that their students aren't broken and don't need to be fixed. They are not there to become clones of the teacher, spouting the same facts and ideas, nor to be convinced of anything. Students have inquiring minds, seeking to learn how to think, how to sharpen the reasoning faculty, and become more and more allowing and less and less judgmental. Real education isn't about learning facts as much as it is about learning how to expand one's consciousness and put together new ideas in new ways. When we are taught limitation, constriction, shouldn'ts, can'ts, and only's, then our minds are trapped in endless repetition instead of unending creativity. The greatest **life-**teachers aren't necessarily the ones with the most students. They are the ones who create the greatest number of teachers of independent thinking and feeling.

Religions have convinced millions that it's better to give than receive. Yet the Self is crying out for its turn to be Number One. Please, ME. We have learned to suppress these yearnings to pay homage to social customs. Yet the Self will not be denied. It wants to be noticed. It wants to receive. It wants to be first or at least equal.

Hence we seek escape from this oppression and self-denial. In its most unhealthy form, we manifest dis-ease, self-victimizing situations, addictions, gangs, thrill-seeking and other attention-getting devices. The body ultimately pays the toll on its self-imposed denial. It gets sick. It seeks solace in substances that suppress these feelings. It ends up with mates that abuse it to match the low self-worth the body has been taught.

Religious leaders teach an origin of low self-worth using the concept of Original Sin. In this belief, not only do we have to earn God's love and operate according to His rules in order to be worthy, but also we start life with a negative balance sheet. We are already unworthy until we are baptized or in some way have removed this stain that religion itself has imposed on us. This is an amazing teaching. These are time-honored, sacrosanct traditions that are so pervasive and compelling that most people don't even bother to question them. They just accept them because they have given their power away to an institution that says it gets its authority from God. Such beliefs are usually taught from childhood. In fact, those who do question the teachings are often isolated, shunned, humiliated, shamed and guilted into compliance, silence or submission and even tried, convicted and excommunicated by the judgment of a religious court.

Religions can perform a most valuable service in leading individuals to experience God. They also offer community and a place and time to focus on gratitude and awareness of all creation. Religion serves best when it leads to enlightenment and the experience of love. Most experiences, however, fall sadly short of such a noble effort. Instead, they offer a rigid set of rules, shoulds, limitations, laws and punishments leading to fear of a mighty and terrible, judgmental and conditionally loving being. Is there a victim somewhere in this scenario? If so, it is obvious that such an institution is a creation out of fear and not out of love.

Those who embrace these fear-based beliefs later in life as adults do so out of a deep and compelling need to find some system of beliefs to rescue them from their fears of separation from God and their own perceived unworthiness. They believe that this new system of behavior, the chosen religion, has the power to show them the way out of their isolation and self-hatred, away from their unnamed fears about life and the afterlife.

A friend once said, "Religion is for people who are fearful of going to hell. Spirituality is for people who've been through their hell and are seeking the way back." Please understand, there is no blame in any of these choices. We are endowed with inalienable free will and blessed with an unconditional Father-Mother God-Goddess. We ourselves are our only judge, no other.

If people would ask themselves how a completely unconditionally loving God could possibly ever see them as less than perfect creations, no matter what they have done or might do, then they would realize that love of self, the reflection of the love of God, Creator, Spirit, All that Is, Oneness, already perceives them as perfect and thus, they can too. They are already worthy of the whole universe just by the fact that they exist. They already are an expression of inestimable value because they are a piece, an aspect, of Creator.

Walt had been struggling with religion since his church had excommunicated him after 48 years of constant and faithful service. Ten years prior, while married, he had cuddled, hugged and kissed a woman who was not his wife when he had been away from home for many months. He disclosed this to his mate who said, "You'll never be right with God unless you confess this to the church." So he did. His pastor couldn't deal with it and passed him off to his superior. Again Walt was forced to humiliate himself by dredging up every last minute detail of this ten-year-old infraction. This high church official said, "Since you had a position of authority, you must be punished even more severely than others. We will hold a trial."

At that point, Walt said "NO! I've done enough. I've confessed, humbled myself, long ago repented and asked for forgiveness. I will not repeat this story ever again. You may hold a trial if you want, but I won't be there. I've had enough public shame and guilt and judgment for my long ago minimal infraction."

The church held that trial with 12 men who didn't even know Walt and they excommunicated him. Walt disclosed his well thought out conclusion. "If we only live for about 80 years (his church didn't believe in reincarnation), a short span of time in relationship to all eternity, and if we goof up in that short span of time, how could a loving God possibly condemn us to an endless and everlasting hell for millions and billions of years for our human, god-given fallibility?"

As parents, we wouldn't do this to our own child, so how could God? Walt had awakened. No longer was he a victim of a judgmental God. He knew himself as a creator and God as Love.

Those who evidence low self-worth are constantly looking for a rescuer to show them in some way they are acceptable and worthy of kindness, good things, a prosperous and healthy life, encouragement and praise. Because we do not know how to find worth inside ourselves, and we seek it externally, we create our reality in the world around us as a reflection of the degree of worthlessness we feel inside. Hence, we may get into a string of abusive relationships or take a series of low-paying jobs.

Remember, 'as within, so without'. If you feel yourself to be unworthy of approval for your skill at your job, you will create myriad people to reflect that. Your boss will ignore your efforts. Your coworkers will sabotage you. With your low self-worth being validated, you will begin to make errors, fall behind, be late, or subconsciously find other ways to confirm that you are a poor worker. In its final stages, this behavior leads to being passed over for promotion, perceived discrimination, a workplace lawsuit or injury, or being fired. Victims wait for a rescuer in order to get relief. They do not see that they are capable of changing their reality and creating a world they prefer. As long as they wait for action to begin outside them, they will only create more victimhood. It is easy to see which Triad these people are working from. As we continue, it becomes easier and easier to use this tool to see the true dynamics at play.

Exercise to Stop Seeing Yourself as a Victim

Pay attention for one hour at a time to what comes out of your mouth. Really hear what you are saying that reflects your perception of not being in charge in your life. Note in which part of the Fear triangle you are playing. Note the emotional state as you hear yourself say such self-defeating statements as, "My spouse won't let me _____," "I can't be successful because of _____," or "I can't take any time for myself because _____."

Then reverse the victim role you were playing. Rephrase your limitations so they become statements of your choices and your power such as "I choose to _____," "I will be (am) successful because _____," or "I am taking time for myself by _____."

Exercise: Diagram the above situations in terms of the Triads.

Manifesting Low Self-Worth

Recently, a client came to me with carpal tunnel syndrome and internal injuries aggravated by prolonged sitting. She swears she loves her job of typing transcriptions on a computer for eight hours a day, yet her body is clearly saying, "You didn't get the message when your higher self said no more of this. You didn't get it when you thought about starting your own company. You didn't get it when you tried to commit suicide because your emotions had given out. So it has finally appeared on the physical level, in its densest form of communication, one you can't ignore."

And so she doesn't merely ignore it, she denies it. She refuses to see that her carpal tunnel pain is caused by her dislike of what she is doing. She lives in her head, and refuses to acknowledge that the problem is her low self-esteem and her fear of joblessness. It's obvious to everyone but her that she has choices and is not really stuck. She has options but chooses to block all possibilities that conflict with her own low opinion of her self-worth. Illness will be her excuse until she wakes up and sees that there are other choices, and that she is worthy of having them. Her carpal tunnel is her body's message that she no longer wishes to handle this situation and is losing her flexibility.

Fear of Lack

Fear of Lack can be applied to the simplest of situations. We fear not getting the window seat on the plane or our mate eating the last piece of chocolate cake we were saving for ourself. We fear not getting what we want, when we want it, in the way we want it.

This fear paralyzes us when it is a profound physical threat such as starvation or homelessness. Not only can it be fear of lacking the resources for physical survival, but the threat of lack of stature in a prosperous nation wherein value is determined by wealth and power. Fear of lack crops up in numerous instances daily. We are so used to feeding this fear that we hardly notice it.

This quite natural fear often drives people who hate their jobs to remain in them, claiming they work to pay the bills. There is no life except work. Then, too, a well-paid and seemingly successful executive may have the same fear and hates her job but is owned by the big salary and benefits. She is fearful of leaving, fearful that such income could never be replaced and her lifestyle requires all she earns and more.

I remember a time during my financial fiasco when each month felt worse than the last. It wasn't a question of whether a loss would take place but one of how much. Walking across a grocery store parking lot one afternoon, I was suddenly struck by the realization that I didn't even have the money to buy groceries and could literally starve to death. Each month's business expenses exceeded income by $50,000. The absolute paralyzing fear of that moment was etched on my emotional body. The terror of it ran its course of adrenaline from head to toe. I owned my poverty. I owned my fear of lack. I froze in mid-step, terrified. I envisioned living on the streets, or in a shelter, the daily grind being looking for ways to eat, going on welfare, being trapped by powerlessness. I said to my then husband, "We don't have any money for food." He replied, "We'll always have money for food."

His reassurance opened a doorway in the terror and my senses came back on-line. I started breathing again. I heard what he'd said, truly heard. I knew I'd be okay, at least regarding food and the basic necessities for survival.

But the bloodletting was far, far from over. It continued for years after that time. Before and during the financial devastation, I had severe lower back problems, typical of financial worries, I've since learned. Remember, all dis-ease is based in our emotions and reflected in our body as each blockage, fear and stress percolates up to the surface. All fears and judgments show up in our physical body eventually. Lower back pain most often reflects fear of lack of economic support because the spinal cord holds the body erect. When the body is not feeling supported, physically, emotionally, mentally or spiritually, the fear shows up as a lower back weakness since the spine itself represents support. (For more on the connection between emotional or mental stresses and how they affect the physical body, see Louise Hay's many wonderful books.)

Fear of Control or Lack of Control

This fear is extremely insidious, hiding behind and masquerading in the subtle manipulation of others, supposedly for their benefit. In truth, the controller usually has an unacknowledged agenda. We fear taking control and being responsible for making decisions that may turn out badly for us and others as much as we fear others making choices for us that can't guarantee our preferred outcome.

Children on the Playground

It's really valuable to look at any given situation using the analogy of children on a playground and seeing those involved acting out parts. Would they be the shy child, the neighborhood bully, the flirt, the wounded child, the teacher's pet, the goody-goody, or the attention getter? Disengaged from the charged atmosphere of the adult experience, we can see the simplified dynamics of the interaction and more easily interpret and defuse the emotions.

Playground behaviors do not necessarily go away when we grow to adulthood. They simply transform into more acceptable adult characteristics. The coworker who is always getting hurt is still the little kid getting a banged knee or scraped elbow, who is vulnerable, wants attention and doubtless unwittingly, plays a victim role. Adults who choose long-distance or married lovers would be the schoolyard kids who can't approach the person they adore, suggesting either shyness or woundedness. These childhood emotional states will be the operating systems creating their adult worlds and they will constantly wonder why they never seem to have that ideal relationship that lives in their heads, installed there by faulty programmers called 'society'. Having been so programmed, adults believe their perceptions to be reality and there is no control over them. Their instilled subconscious emotions are running the show.

One of the great fears of our society is the fear of being out of control. It is psychologically beaten into us as children. How many thousands of times during the first five years of our lives do we hear "Control yourself." or "Don't do that!"? No wonder we try to control ourselves and everything around us. The constant admonition to "Control yourself" is associated with everything from our bathroom elimination to showing and expressing our feelings around others. In fact, it begins while the child is in diapers with toilet training that child experts recognize as a serious, potentially traumatic experience.

Look at this next situation. Your teenage son plans to take the car to the mall. You ask him to call you when he gets there. This may seem like the caring parent but, on closer inspection, it is a controlling one. Yes, I know, you may feel this is about his being responsible. Really it's about *your* fears and *your* need not to worry. You make him responsible for your feelings and you ride herd on him until he does. You are demanding he give up control to you. I'm not saying don't care. Ask him what your requirements feel like and he'll probably tell you about your control issues. You are the persecutor to his victim. Your worry is your issue. Remember, no one can make you feel anything. I'm suggesting that if a parent had allowed him some control and decision-making ability earlier, instead of constantly overprotecting him, then you would either feel complete confidence in his ability or he would volunteer to call you out of consideration for your normal anxieties. We all have the right to make a wrong decision. What's one of the main reasons kids want to leave home? To be able to make their own decisions!

Kira sent her 17-year-old daughter, Sonja, to me for counseling. Sonja's first complaint was, "I don't have any space at home that's mine. If I'm reading a book, I can't leave it on my desk because my mother makes me put it away. I can't paint because she makes me put away all my paints and canvases every day. She came into my bedroom and rearranged the furniture because she wanted it different. I have to get out so I can be me."

Sonja had already run away twice and was hanging out with friends her mother didn't approve of, trying to create a sense of independence. She wanted control of her own life. If her mother had given her independence in previous years, things would have been very different. She was hanging on to control too tightly, afraid Sonja could not handle even simple aspects of her own life.

Take the example of the business executive who won't delegate anything because she can do it faster, more impressively, and get better results. This is a more obvious example of the need for control and fear of its lack. If she could learn how to delegate and give up the need for micro management, she would actually discover there are others who may be even better at the task than she is. By continuing the tight control, she misses the opportunity of finding and training superior employees and also doesn't have to deal with the possibility of feeling inferior herself. As in this example, most situations are a combination of several fears and can involve all three roles in the Fear Triad.

Executive in Control

Rita was a high-powered executive who plotted, war-gamed, agenda-ized, laid out, and goal-oriented every situation in her life, including her emotions and personal relationships. She was in terror of just allowing the situation to unfold. She managed social events to retain control of who should talk to whom and on what subject. If she left the room, she gave instructions as to what could or couldn't be talked about in her absence. When she re-entered the same room, she made a dramatic entrance, grabbing the attention and shifting the topic, no matter what it was, in order to control every last piece of conversation. It was almost impossible to be around her for any length of time because no matter what the topic, she would cut in to the conversation by changing it, or stating she needed to find a restroom, or mentioning something she was looking at, or recalling something to tell you. She simply could not stop the controlling. This was all to cover up her own insecure feelings. She was in danger of losing control because of unresolved deep-seated grief and loss.

To stem the tidal wave, she kept extremely busy, lived life on the financial edge, kept an agenda that would bring most executives to their knees and manipulated her personal life to fit into that world at arm's length. Little by little, with counseling, she began feeling safe enough to release the need for control in her personal life. She did it by learning to see how much she was manipulating and paid attention to these awarenesses. One of her most enlightening realizations was that she would second-guess how her lover would respond in a situation and then produce a calculated reaction based on that assumption.

When she realized what she was doing, she was amazed. She is letting go, little by little. A highly intelligent and capable woman, she realizes that feeling safe within herself is how she will move forward.

Hiring a Champion

My life's issue has been control. Feeling that I'm better at doing something, I wouldn't let anyone else do it. I could get the result I wanted more easily, cheaper, better, whatever. I had to be in control. As my investments began to crash, I realized something else was going on. I asked, "Why? Why is this happening? How did I create it? How do I use metaphysical principles to fix it?"

During a counseling session, Rajni said, "Give up control; hire a champion."

"Sure," I replied smugly, "and just who's big enough and has enough ability to step in and manage all the financing, negotiations and lenders?"

Raj simply said, "Think big."

So in a smart alec tone, I said, "Fine, the President of the United States!"

Raj said, "Think a little smaller."

Bingo! I had it! A congressman! Isn't that their job, to champion for the little people? So I did let go. I talked with our local congressman and his aide handled the whole thing. Since the properties were in the inner city area, it was to his advantage to champion decent housing for the low-income residents. He called a meeting of all the government people I couldn't get to talk to me, to coordinate, or to be reasonable. They were all required to travel 45 miles to our location where he had staged the conference. I was amazed. The aide told me I was not to speak, but to just listen. This was definitely a demonstration about control.

As the meeting began, I looked at the attendees. They were quite subdued, quiet and patient. Just a week ago, these same people had been overbearing, accusatory, attacking and game-playing. As the congressman's aide began speaking, his words carried power and they listened obediently. I sat there thinking, *I'd sure like to tell them* _____ and, lo and behold, the aide said those very words, his position and power carrying far more weight than mine ever could have. I was amazed.

Then I thought, *They need to hear* _____ and, lo and behold, he said that very thing. After the ninth time this happened, I sat stunned and deliriously overjoyed, but not showing any overt emotion. After all, I was still in control.

When the meeting was over, the attendees were summarily dismissed and I had no further problem with that office. Knowing for real, experientially, that I did not have to be in control to get things done was so satisfying and so energizing. I knew the universe would show me the ways to release my need for that control. Finally I began to understand there was a higher power to align with that stayed in tune with my greatest good. It was a memorable step on my "let go and let God" journey. I could now focus on other things rather than my fear of lack of control. I had found a way to stop being a victim of their behavior.

Recognizing Patterns in Our Lives

Not again! It was my fourth relationship with an alcoholic. Oh, they weren't the falling down drunk kind or the abusive kind, just men in need of more drinks and then more drinks. People drink to excess to extinguish fear and feelings. My husband had become alcoholic over time. I don't remember his being that way in the very beginning but, by the early 1980s, I found myself calling a toll-free number from a television ad for an alcoholic treatment center. I was in tears and at the end of my rope.

I didn't know what I had done. Where did I go wrong? What had I said or done to make him do this? I felt such horrible guilt. When I called the number, the right person was there, saying just the right things and I heard her. "Listen to me," she said. "You have not done anything to cause this. This is not your fault. This is his problem."

She then asked, "How often does this occur?" and quickly determined that he had a drinking problem. It was a shock to me but

I somehow knew she was right. I saw everything from a different perspective. I would be supportive and try to help. I was never a nag, so I didn't harp on the subject. Years passed. I discovered the meaning of enabling and terms like codependency and saw how I was actually part of the problem but still I made few comments. I suggested he needed help but he was in great denial. It was affecting our relationship but he couldn't see it. I finally told him, "I won't nag but, one day, I'll just be gone."

He promised to 'be good' and stop drinking to prove he didn't have a problem for a couple months, but always the same or worse addiction would return. Finally, I left.

Then the first man I dated after I left was from a family of six children, all alcoholics. He was never really drunk, just always got himself to the point of feeling good every night. He couldn't finish an evening without one or two beers and kept asking me, "Do you think I have a drinking problem?"

I'd say, "You're the one who has to figure that out, but you keep wondering. You might want to look at that."

Next came a boyfriend who'd gotten a DWI and still denied he had a problem. Then, a relationship with a sweet guy who had half a dozen hard alcoholic drinks a day but I was naive enough to think that his "cokes" were really just cola. He'd pour a coke with lots of ice, but I didn't know he also added a generous slug of vodka. Looking back, I am amazed at my blindness and stupidity.

Then I became angry with myself. Why was I doing this? Why was I creating alcoholics in my life? If they had been drug users, I wouldn't have tolerated them for a moment. If they'd been sloppy, embarrassing drunks, I would have left immediately. I was obviously selecting a narrow cross-section of addiction. I was an enabler in some way. But how? And why?

I went to a counselor but he was rude, arrogant and simply said, "Given that you have high expectations, your choices are limited to two percent of the male population and since you will have a hard time finding a mate, you'd better take what you can get."

I was so livid I determined to find the answer to why I displayed this pattern. I had gotten no clue, no insights and no help from this 'professional' so, after demanding an answer from the universe I went to Melanie, a spiritual counselor, and finally found out. She said, "We choose a mate with such a flaw because it allows us to remain in control, to be better than."

Bingo! Control once again—of my feelings, of situations, of whatever I was in contact with. I could always do everything better and faster, so why not control it. I'd proven I was right in my business life. I seemed definitely and respectably in control but I was, in truth, out of control, way overboard and totally unaware of it.

Melanie added, "The person who drinks is out of control to some degree. By comparison, it allows your non-aggressive control tendencies to be validated and, by default, puts you in control, because your mate obviously isn't. You don't have to wrest control from him because by selecting such a mate, you are invited to be the controller."

This meant that I was still unwilling to surrender to feelings, just like alcoholics who drink for the most part so that they don't have to feel. Therefore, with this as a mirror, I realized that this was my payoff: by choosing an alcoholic, I was insuring that my mate wasn't going to feel his feelings, and therefore that I didn't have to either. Nor did I have to deal with those nasty little sensations that I perceived as weakness my feelings.

Asking for Emotional Help

I decided to change, to feel. For the first time ever, I actually asked for emotional help one day when I really needed it. It was the day of my divorce. I was hurting, feeling raw and needed a shoulder to lean on. I went to see my friend Jerry and said, "I just came from court and got my divorce. I need to be loved, nurtured and cared for."

I was truly overwhelmed. For the first time in my life, I was asking for emotional help. Bless his heart, Jerry was totally present for me.

He put down what he was doing, turned towards me and said, "I'm here for you. What would you like?"

I was shocked. So one didn't die of embarrassment at expressing a feeling. It could be survived. The reason for my trepidation was that, in my family, expressing sentiment brought invalidation, humiliation, shame and embarrassment. Crying was absolutely just asking for the worst kind of contempt and mockery. But with Jerry, I realized that people could actually be compassionate when you expressed emotions. I didn't have to rescue, or be strong for, everyone else. Someone might be there for me and my feelings. Someone else could be in control and just let me feel. All this was new to me and hit me in a flash. But now I was waking up and I was conscious of thinking all this and of feeling it!

Next, a wonderful, highly intelligent man came into my life. He had many personal problems, but at least he wasn't an alcoholic. Then the next two men I was attracted to were homosexual. I needed to rethink this whole thing! But at least I was working my way through my control issue and no longer resisting my feelings. I knew this because the gay men in these two situations were willing to explore their feelings in their own relationships and also no more alcoholics came into my life. When I was truly ready to look at this situation, and own my part in creating it, I healed it.

Then I met the wonderful man who is now my life mate. He could count on one hand the times he's had an alcoholic drink, is in touch with all his feelings and is able to freely talk about them. At last.

Taking True Control

Being able to tap into our feelings in any given moment is evidence of true and authentic self control. It is the control that doesn't need control. It is the art of being in touch with your self. If a frog is thrown into hot water, its reflexes will cause it to jump out immediately. But if a frog is put into a pan of cold water on a stove and the water is gradually brought to a boil, it will allow itself to be boiled alive. This shows us the value of paying attention to the present moment, of not slipping into passivity but staying conscious and asking ourselves each step of the way, "How do I feel?" If you don't feel comfortable in a situation, change what you can.

Fear of Change

The question is, how can we sense the heat is being turned up when we don't recognize our situation (job, relationship, health, habits, etc.) as becoming uncomfortable and aren't even looking for it? Denial and unawareness is much easier than disconnecting from or changing circumstances even when they become painful. We've adapted, like the frog, to the gradual discomfort. To change our behavior is fearsome and to look at oneself and feel those emotions demanding change even more so. So we remain stuck, readjusting our comfort levels until we come face to face with ourselves or we let circumstances do it for us.

Making Changes Safely

The same is true for weight gain. We don't realize we are becoming large until one day we catch ourselves unaware in a mirror or someone says, "Hey, fatty." We are asleep so much of our lives. How do we muster the courage to wake up and, if we do, how do we effect change? Where is the motivation? Health concerns (really fear of illness)? Lovers' opinions (really self-worth issues)? All this is just fear. There must be a positive and healthy motivator for change to be lasting. It finally happens when we say, "I've had enough!"

The desire to discover behavior patterns that brought us to the point of no return is the first motivator to waking up on the journey to self. Finding the patterns is the second step. Then removing judgment from them and oneself is the third. Having a supportive, empowering (not enabling) relationship with a friend, counselor, lover, mate or group is a huge asset. Relying on our own connection to divinity through our own guidance is our grandest asset and this creates a passion for the inward journey.

Sometimes we just come to love ourselves as we are when change seems impossible or the passion for change evaporates. Finally, we realize the unhealthy, co-dependent, unloving, self-destructive habits that filled our emotional void and learn to replace them with healthy habits worthy of our new selves. We can do this when we are aware, awake and then choose to do it.

We can be way-showers for others. We can be willing to be vulnerable and journey through our personal process without retreat from our fears. In viewing our process, others can see a choice to take their own inward journey. We cannot do the work for them. Each must do his or her own work, and follow his or her own path. And they all come to such an awareness when it is in their highest and best interest to do so, not ours.

Running a Business on Metaphysical Principles: Control without Control

Just prior to my business crash, my need for control was exhibited in my persistent search for a bank that could fund my real estate portfolio. After all those loan rejections I still persisted, oblivious to obvious inner guidance, which I denied, not to mention external signals that things were not working and this was not my highest path. I was still being very transmissive (intensely determined to do, direct, accomplish) and overcome all obstacles according to my plan, no matter how formidable they seemed. I had been both counseling clients and doing the investment business for four years. One day I recognized that my 'job' as an investor had ended. I could no longer purchase, finance or rehab properties and my staff was already doing the day-to-day management. I simply closed up my desk and shifted all my attention to doing psychic readings.

When I began my career in metaphysical work, I applied this same transmissive attitude. I believed that in order to continue in the face of rejections, one had to have fortitude, goal focus, stick to it-ive-ness, fearlessness—or so it seemed. Society validated this kind of conduct. After all, the American dream was built on such determination. However, I found a different and equally powerful way—listening. I learned that if I listened to the obvious "no's," I could allow a different path to appear that was in my highest and best good. This let me align my goals with God's. I stopped having to be in charge, having to be right and needing to have it be my way.

To walk our talk is difficult in any way of living. It is, however, more visible in its success or failure in certain areas, especially one teaching the basic principles of existence. In many businesses, we can easily find power trips, territorializing, "pedestaling," jealousy and backbiting. Although those are found routinely in the business world, I somehow expected higher standards for the 'business' of metaphysics.

I wondered if it could really be done. I have always felt that if you can't run a metaphysical business based on metaphysical principles, then it cannot be done anywhere. I would allow it to unfold. So I structured my business on my principles of existence.

First, I would not let "should's" enter my business. If I desire to do something, I will. If I do not wish to do something and am only doing it because it's a should, then I won't do it. For instance, as I sat relaxed in a bookstore, I would think, "*I should call the office*". Since that was a "should," I decided not to call. Later I'd say to myself, "*I think I'll call the office.*" Since it was no longer a "should," I called. I did this process for an hour a day, then two, then three and finally four hours a day until I broke the "should" habit.

Second, I would listen for guidance from the universe. The following story illustrates how we can safely change our old habits by listening to that small voice within that has our best interests at heart, even if it doesn't seem like it at first.

When starting my new psychic business, I wanted to get a banner made for display at psychic fairs. I had only three weeks and limited funds to prepare for a large Canadian fair. I thought it would be easy. I called a sign company out of the phone book.

"No problem," the man said. "We can do that for you in plenty of time for only $65."

"Great!" I said, "Will you be there for 20 minutes till I can get there?"

"Yes, I'll wait." he replied.

I jumped in the car. When I arrived, his wife was there instead. I introduced myself and she went stiff. "No, we can't do that for 3 weeks. We're booked. And it will cost $195."

I couldn't figure out what had happened until I realized that she disliked psychics and that's what my banner would read. I was shocked but trusted the universe and continued to look for the another company. I'd always done that in my business; just solve the problem. I was proud that I didn't get angry.

Though blocked, I became as before, single-minded, determined, and kept looking. After four more attempts at various sign companies, all were unsatisfactory in some way. The last place I looked was the most expensive. Now I was really frustrated. I only had three more days until the fair. Finally, I got the message! The universe was telling me not to do this; to let it go and forget about the sign and go with the flow. I didn't know why I needed to stop this search but realized that I had been transmissive, that is, my male side was directing me to *take action and solve the problem.* That's what I'd done my entire business life and it was time to change. I had considered myself to be a problem solver but what does a problem solver need to maintain her identity? More problems! What a trap! So I let go of that. But I still didn't know why the Universe was telling me to change directions about the banner. Was it because there would be no space for it at the fair? Or would it need to be changed and I was being saved the expense? I didn't need to know right then. I just needed to trust the Universe and I did.

Two days before leaving for Canada, I went to a party and I learned the hostess had just lost her job. Another guest entered the room and, as she passed the bookshelf, an album fell off. "What's this?" the guest asked, picking it up.

"Photos of the banners I used to make for people for fairs," the hostess replied.

My mouth dropped open. The awareness of Spirit's hand in this was stunning and joy-filled. I hired her on the spot to make my banner. Not only did she now have time do it, but she was so good she could finish it in two days. She could really use the money and best of all, her price was more than fair and affordable.

She gathered samples and made suggestions as to fabrics. I gave her my business card and asked her basically to copy it. The result was stunning and led to many other jobs for her. It was a win-win situation. Going with the flow is proving to be a good idea, I thought. This metaphysical stuff really works.

Third, when the push to get everything done for the start up of this business became too much and I wasn't having fun, I stopped. Life is to be enjoyed, I believed, and not to be made stressful. I took many breaks. I could see how easy it would be to fall back into old patterns of workaholic and overachiever, and vowed, "Never again." I decided to choose joy. It really is always an option.

Next, I chased down several companies who made posters. These costs skyrocketed, too, so again I let go and someone in my class turned out to be a professional graphics designer and offered to do the posters in exchange for the class fees. So it too was done on time, professionally and beautifully, in grace and ease.

Then I realized I needed an artist's portfolio for carrying the posters. By then I just allowed the universe to provide. The graphics designer had an old one she was about to throw out which she gave me.

The large easel I next needed was easily found after allowing it to come to me instead of "pushing the river." By now I'd gotten the message and was in the flow. The business cards and the logo design came just as easily. I received the design and layout in a meditation. The business cards which were originally $400 ended up less than $85. Giving up control was really working.

Since then, I have continued to let the universe provide for me, for it is eminently qualified and capable of doing so. Prosperity and abundance are our natural heritage, and we have but to allow them in. I was learning that I could let go of my need to control.

The same principle works in minor everyday business things. Let it flow and recognize that when you misdial, get a busy tone, or lose the phone number, you are being guided by your higher self not to contact that person at that time. You don't have to know why; just realize that you are already connected to the best guidance possible, so stop judging an event as good or bad, failure or not, and *go with the flow*. It will then work out to your advantage.

Fear of Separation

The fear of separation is a fear about change. Change may run the gamut from school graduation, job change, marriage, entering puberty, all the way to divorce or death. The body registers change as an end to existing conditions. The degree of our fear of that ending determines the impact of it on our lives. Often our emotions reflect them in our dreams, perhaps a dream of a funeral when big changes are coming, or of our child dying in a traumatic event before he or she graduates from school or moves away from home. Both events are the dying of an old way of being and the birthing of a new way. We may awaken from these dreams fearful and anxious, but this is our own fear of separation from the way we've been living.

All parties involved can experience it. Leaving childhood behind, the onset of puberty often triggers separation fears in the child as well as the parents. Other fears may be triggered also. Fear of lack of control causes the adults in charge to try to prevent or orchestrate the separation. A child leaving home may awaken fear of lack of self-worth in a parent; the empty nest syndrome. The individual dramas are endless.

All separation fears originate in our psyche, our subconscious fears that we are separated from our source, our safety, our Unconditionally Loving Wholeness, God. How can a sunbeam be separate from the sun? How can a shadow be separate from the sun? Both are merely aspects of it. All things are part of Creator. There is no separation. We have just lost our conscious awareness of the bond.

As more and more people have Near-Death Experiences (NDE), clear understanding of this is being brought back into human consciousness. Death as we have always perceived it is not real. Death is just another doorway. Thinking that death is just awful is a trick we play on ourselves because death is so awe-full that, if we really remembered it, we might skip ahead and check out early.

After her divorce, a friend and I had both seen intuitively that her daughter, Chandra, was going to die at age thirteen but we could get no further information on how this would happen. On her 13th birthday, Chandra announced that she was disowning her mother and never wanted to see her again and was moving in with her father. This surely felt like death. Often we cannot explain for certain what some intuitive insights mean. Intuition is not a science but the art of feeling. We feel into a situation and sense its parameters. In this case, we could sense the feeling of an ending, something cut off, finalized, which we interpreted as physical death. However it was a metaphor for the ending of her childhood, their connection and relationship. Truly this was a death to her mother for it would be nine years before her daughter would re-establish the connection after considerable counseling.

My good friend Margaret and I had made a date to spend the day together. I went to the local coffee shop to work on my laptop computer for a couple hours until it was time to meet her. Soon I struck up a conversation with Wayne, also having coffee. Shortly after I was due to meet her, Margaret called to find out where I was. I told her that I was in the middle of a great conversation and asked if it would it be okay to cancel our lunch and afternoon together. She got angry and hung up on me. A few minutes later, she called me back, even angrier, telling me she'd cancelled three client appointments to spend the day with me. I was stunned. I knew she was going through a health crisis and intense emotional upheaval but I still felt as if I weren't allowed to change my mind. I was glad she felt safe enough in our friendship to express her anger rather than stuff it and pretend. I love her authenticity. I knew that, on a less intense day, she would have responded differently. I was in joy and having a great time. Wayne and I talked for over seven hours that day. Meeting him was a wonderful experience.

If I'd told Margaret that I'd had an accident, I would have been forgivable but, since I was having fun with someone else after agreeing to be with her, I was a fair target for her judgment. Any valid reason that involved my having a problem would have made it okay, which is why so many people lie or make up excuses to appear as a victim. This makes being a victim acceptable as an object of rescue. But to stand in one's own power and choose joy, when someone else may be triggered into unhappiness, is not yet acceptable for many.

A separation in our friendship occurred. Could it be repaired? Could we heal it? Would it be different from now on? It was okay for Margaret to get angry—that was real and valid. I had to decide who I was in relationship to that anger. Would I be defensive, allowing, upset, demanding or self-justifying? I could choose. I chose to love her just as she was, anger and all. The separation could be present alongside the friendship. As far as I was concerned, it was just a bump in our connection, not a disconnection. Time has proven the friendship to be as wonderful as ever.

We may react to the drama that unfolds or participate in the drama we create. Choose well. For each of us, the joy of this now and those built upon it depend on our choices.

Shelly came to me saying, "I am rich enough so that I'm never going to get married again." Her concern was that because of her money, she'd never know if her mate loved her for herself or her money. This revealed the fear that she'd be a future victim so she refuses joy in the present in order to protect herself from that fearful potential separation caused by rejection. This is truly a rejection of life.

"You're in your head," I told her. "Get into your feelings and you will know if he is real or not. You're making yourself a victim today so you won't be a victim in the future. You are restricting joy in this now, and this now is all that exists! The fear you flow will create the reality as proof you are right. Begin to shift your focus. Flow love to yourself and learn to trust your feelings. Your path is not about limitation of joy; it is about the journey to the authentic, loveable and totally present you."

So often, people stay out of relationships to avoid damage to self-worth. This is truly a fear of separation multiplied and overlaid with self-worth issues. When Shelly begins to love herself, she will know what real love is and be able to recognize it in others.

Suicide

In the first few weeks of my financial fiasco, I was so emotionally overwhelmed at the collapse of my self-image as one whose word is her bond that I didn't just contemplate suicide; I was on the other side of thinking about it and well into knowing it was real for me. I was coldly and calmly planning the details so as to cause the least impact on others. I know what suicide feels like. It is empty and very much alone. The sense of isolation and hopelessness has no real fear of death. It is just a step, but one I do not advocate. Our transition will most surely come. Meanwhile, since we're in a body, it's important to remember that we chose it, we create our experiences and it is all an illusion. But even the illusions we call feelings seem real, and we most certainly came here to experience them. Life is about being here now. We hear that over and over in new age lingo, but what does it truly mean? It means the richness of all value and worth and experience is here now. So go for it. Suicide ignores the value of being here. It is the belief that somewhere else is better.

The sages teach we all commit suicide. From a higher perspective, all deaths are in truth suicides because they are self-induced and ultimately chosen, for one reason or another. We make the choice that allows for the return of our consciousness to its true home.

Remember we are creators, not just humans being acted upon by an overbearing, decision-making God. In death too we exercise our free will and our subconscious agendas. We are reluctant to admit this because we have equated the worth of a life with longevity. We have disregarded that we are all creators. In fact, we flee from the concept because that would make us responsible for our own life and death. Suicide seems abhorrent to us because we are stuck in judgment of good and bad, win or lose. The conscious taking of one's own life is just a conscious choosing of time and place for transition. It is not being defeated or losing or a waste. It is a choice, akin to quitting a good paying job with all the perks just before retirement—something we judge as bad. But what if that job were killing us through stress and anger, or eating away at our self worth, or sucking all the joy out of us. Slow death. Is that preferable? Is that more honorable or smarter? Is that being self-aware, enlightened? Please understand that I'm not advocating suicide here but am simply freeing it from layers of socialized guilt and judgment in order to look at it differently.

I am simply pointing out that suicide is one of many choices. Does it make sense to choose life in cases of prolonged degenerative, terminal illness? Yes, we can live in hope of a cure. We can also live in hope of a better life next time. Both of these exist in potential futures. I suggest we live in the now instead and make the best-informed choice possible without judgment and allow all others to do likewise.

We may judge that someone's choice to commit suicide is a bad one. It's hard to imagine how any death could be a good thing. But, in truth, there are other considerations, real and valid, such as relief from financial ruin through medical costs, release from horrific pain or removal of the emotional and mental toll on the family. But because we don't want to acknowledge any benefits out of death, we stop the flow of seeing the whole picture as our higher selves would see it in its judgment-free context.

We have been taught that death is not okay, that it means losing and we hate to be losers. But to see how death would be perceived as a gain, ask yourself "How can that be?" Then *remove the judgment* about death and you would begin to understand and feel differently about it. That's what this is all about—feeling and being able to see things from our higher spiritual perspective. Remember, part of this process is to recognize that dying is a divine experience and thus perfect in its very nature.

Recently, a woman in Seattle stopped traffic for four hours while deciding whether or not to jump from a bridge. How do we respond to that? If you were stuck in the traffic jam for four hours, you might judge her act as selfish. If you were related to her, you might judge it as painful. If you were the parent of a child who used the incident to decide not to commit suicide, you might be grateful. We each have our own perspective but can let go and see things from a higher one. We can let go of our need to hang on to feeling injured by someone or something. Otherwise, we make ourselves a victim of the jumper. Each person affected by the jumper has a different perspective. To the mother of the suicidal child, she may be a savior. The woman didn't *do* anything to anyone. She was completely self-absorbed yet she was a trigger for others to choose who they wanted to be in that experience: victim, rescuer or persecutor. Diagramming who is victim and who is persecutor, according to the Triads is an enlightening exercise here. Each participant is playing multiple roles.

Understanding and Overcoming Victimhood

The outstanding characteristic of victims is that they believe someone or something else is responsible, guilty, liable, and the reason for all their experiences. Victims feel powerless. Victims see themselves as less than others and unable to change their circumstances. Victims do not see themselves as having control. Victims don't ask for what they want, feeling they are not worthy of having it. Victims apologize over and over, feeling inadequate and always in the wrong. Victims look to others for direction and point the finger at them as the cause of their pain. Victims are dis-empowered people.

We live in a fear-based, not a love-based culture, which perpetuates victimhood, blame and guilt. Sports, for instance, is based on winning and losing, with losers feeling not good enough, victims of the victors. Court systems, school grades, insurance claims, medical systems, all deal with rescue, judgment and victimization. So do romance and family relations. We seek outside ourselves for reasons and answers to why a thing happened to us. The front page of any newspaper validates this. This approach to life is so well embedded we don't even know how it's running us.

What Are the Consequences of Believing in Victimhood?

First, we can actually become ill. This is the origin of what is called "dis-ease." Dis-ease occurs when we judge and have a negative emotional or mental response to some experience, which is then reflected in the body. The body's normal flow or natural 'ease' ceases and a small, seemingly insignificant block occurs. Over time, like debris caught on a snag in a river, they can become more substantial until serious disruption occurs.

Second, whenever we respond as victims, we are unconsciously giving away a vital part of ourselves—our own personal power. We are saying to the world, "I am not in charge. Someone or something else, bigger or more powerful has control over my life."

Third, we are unconsciously denying that we are Creators and refusing to acknowledge our personal and authentic selves. This dis-empowerment leads us quickly into self judgment. When we feel that something outside ourselves is greater, more powerful and in charge, we bow down to that authority expecting to be judged by it. (And so we are, but by ourselves.) We look to it for guidance. We assume it knows more, is better, that we are not as good and that it is the direct cause of effect in our lives. Sometimes we call it God. Denying responsibility for our own actions then becomes easy.

Fourth, we make God responsible. We judge everything. We make God responsible for making things okay in our lives or not: for denying us what we want, for withholding success from us, for taking away who or what we love, or for not intervening when we need help and generally, for dispensing or withholding blessings. God becomes both our rescuer and persecutor. We become insignificant, impotent and sinful. To win the favor of this capricious being, we adopt a structure of rules and laws to follow. We have truly made God human instead of making ourselves a reflection of the Creator.

When we ask, "Why would God do this to me?" or "Why doesn't God save me from this crisis?" both questions imply we are victims, that someone *could* do something *to* us and that someone *should* do something *for* us. Both reflect the belief that there is an ominous and omnipotent power over us and that we are victims in need of saving.

Suppose God loves unconditionally. Such a God could never see us as victims. There would be, therefore, no need for rescue. Instead, endowed by God with free will to create as we see fit, we are creators. God is unconditionally allowing of all our creations: illnesses, abuses, joys and sorrows. Unconditionally! Everything we could possibly ever do, including all our "judge-able offences" are totally acceptable to an unconditionally loving being who honors us as creators experiencing our reality with unlimited free will. As such, we are free of judgment to create freely, without limitation, without interference and are lovingly supported in ALL our choices, however negative they may seem to us.

A conditional, humanistic God was created from fearful victim thinking. Man had forgotten he could never be disconnected from his Source and lost the knowledge of his creator abilities. In order to explain reality and seeking power in their role as intercessor between man and God, religious leaders taught that a capricious God punished or rewarded man. From this fear, laws regarding conduct and morals were created. Unconditional in his love, God makes no rules to be judged by. The Ten Commandments is an affirmation by God, greatly edited and misinterpreted, that when you have learned unconditional love, these ten things will no longer tempt or distract you.

I know this sounds like license to do anything we please, no matter how bad. But when we know ourselves as empowered creators, when we see ourselves as love, loving and loved, we will consistently choose, *without the need for rules,* the highest action in alignment with our highest self. In other words, our life will proceed out of our highest God-aligned self. "Bad" actions proceed from our unconscious self which is unaware and does not know it is already love. So it creates out of fear. Result? Victim.

Victim Consciousness

Just what is victim consciousness? We instantly resist being labeled a victim unless it serves us in some manner. *If we resist something, react to it, or deny it, we're giving energy to it and it is indeed one of our issues.* If it is something we ponder, laugh off, or just allow to pass through us, it's not our issue.

Resistance tends to push away what we don't want to own or look at but *what we resist persists* because the universe responds by giving us more of what we give energy to. So then we become master wall builders, erecting huge, thick barriers of resistance around the parts of ourselves we don't want revealed. We feel violated if someone gets past our defenses and touches our hidden fears and doubts. We don't want to be vulnerable. But deep inside we all want someone to know all those secrets and still love us. Our resistance to facing things is greatest when we fear that if someone knows the real us, we will no longer be included, approved of or accepted.

Suppose someone said, "You have the ugliest green hair I've ever seen!" Because you are absolutely sure that you don't have green hair, you would look at the person and try to figure out what he or she meant, or chuckle at it, or let it go, because it has no connection to your perceptions of yourself. But, if someone says, "What happened to your face?" you may instantly put your hand up to hide that one pimple, facial hair, mole, scar, or whatever disturbs you.

If you find yourself reacting, defending or denying something in this way, then the item it is still an issue for you. You have just become a victim of yourself and your own self-judgments, your perception of unlovability, or poor self-worth. Yes, the other person was a trigger, but you choose to react in victimhood consciousness or stay centered in your knowing regarding the truth or illusion of the situation. Whatever you judge negatively is what you have not yet loved about yourself.

How Do We Stop Being Victims?

We stop being a victim by making a choice. It's not difficult, but it is a learned, rather than automatic, behavior. We can begin to create new healthy habits. We have already described how you create everything that happens to you and everything that happens in your reality. Why not learn how you can create what you prefer and then choose a new and more joy-filled experience?

Choosing Allowance

Mr. Tate owed me money for equipment purchased. His payments had stopped and he didn't respond to friendly collection efforts. Having been on the "harassee" side of things before, I didn't want to be the vile collector. After nine monthly letters and no reply, my partner and I visited Mr. Tate, some 60 miles away, one winter evening. The house was dark and showed no evidence of being occupied. A FOR SALE sign was in the driveway. I banged on the door and used the rapper heavily. It opened. "Good evening, Mr. Tate," I said. "I'm Dolly, the lady you bought the equipment from."

"Yes, yes, hello," he replied, stepping outside in his pajamas and quickly closing the door behind him. I was amazed he remembered me. "I stopped by to pick up the equipment you purchased," I told him.

"Oh yes, I'm so sorry about that. My wife didn't tell me about it and I've been out of the country. It's in storage but I'll bring it to you tomorrow with the delinquent amount."

Having been a landlord for eons, I could read between the lines and his body language shouted "liar," and Mr. Tate was quite accomplished. My partner wanted to give him the benefit of the doubt. Although I felt Mr. Tate was lying, I choose the higher path of politeness and allowance and upon leaving, jotted down the realtor's phone number on the For Sale sign. I called immediately. "Oh I'm so sorry," she said, "the house is sold and is closing at the end of the week."

The next morning, Mr. Tate appeared at my home, equipment in hand. While patting his coat front he began his story with, "I'm so sorry I realized halfway here that I'd driven off without my checkbook". He developed this fairy tale with great emotion, saying, "I'll have to apply for a loan to pay the past due, and my wife kept all this hidden from me. We've had considerable words over this and I'm not sure about the effect it's had on our relationship."

On and on he went, quite the accomplished victim for whom I should now feel great sympathy, but I'd seen many people try this act and he wasn't taking home any Oscars for his performance. My patience was wearing thin when he made a fatal mistake. "What about proceeds from the sale of your home?" I asked.

"Oh no, it's been for sale for six months; it'll never sell."

Now I was angry, for I had proof he'd lied and had no intention of paying. I decided to place a lien on his home and notified his realtor. Here I had to make a decision. What emotional state would I be in while taking this action? If I did it out of anger, a great deal of focus would be on getting revenge, proving a point, being a persecutor rescuing myself from victimhood and finally making a victim of him. Since I knew that energy creates and what you focus on you get more of, I needed to be aware of my focus in this process. The old me would clearly create a persecutor-victim-rescuer reality, definitely operating in the Fear Triad.

But I didn't want to be a victim driven by my own fears about the energy I might be creating here. What to do? I meditated and got clear that if I let go of the need for an outcome in my favor, stayed true to a common sense business practice and removed any victim energy, then I would be in a healthy space. If it were in my highest and best interest to place the lien, then when I initiated it, things would flow easily. But if they did not, then it would not be in my highest and best interest and I wouldn't force it. I let go of the need for a particular outcome. I stopped breathing heavily. My pulse rate went down. The tension left my shoulders.

The next morning, I simply gathered all the necessary information. It all came easily, each step of the way. And so it flowed and got done. I let go and totally forgot about it. A week later, the escrow agent called requesting the amount due as she would be paying it off in closing. End of story.

I feel certain that if I had carried the energy of revenge into the process, it would not have had such a positive conclusion. By staying in allowance, I was true to my knowing that an honest debt was owed. I was not a victim here *nor* was Mr. Tate.

Breaking the Victim/Persecutor Paradigm

Victimhood is like a comfortable, known behavior, an old knee jerk response and is often, "You hurt me, so I'll hurt you back." When we realize that *you* equals me, that we are one, and what you do to the least of my brethren, you do unto self, then we will shift. When we consciously choose to change our re-actions in any given situation, we begin to create a new healthy pattern. We come from our centered selves and act instead of re-act. This I call being centered-in-self. It is not self-centered. We learn to come from that centered place within, rather than from our unbalanced and needy ego. We then break the victim paradigm.

A lady in an interracial marriage came to me for help. Her large front window had been broken for the third time and she wanted me to psychically name the culprit from her list of three teenage suspects. Then she would sue the parents of the unfortunate and misguided youngster. Instead, the reading became a counseling session about why she was experiencing victim consciousness, perceiving attacks and needing revenge. She began to see the intensity of her energy's focus was on negativity. She had created separatism and hatred within herself. She had built walls around her heart and felt everyone was her persecutor. She was now experiencing such enmity between herself and her mate.

She left my office a changed woman, aware that she was creating and not just being violated and victimized. She understood how she was drawing such actions to her by the passion and intensity of her fears. She had not accepted herself as lovable. She saw her children as targets of bi-racial attack. She began to shift her thinking away from fear and victimhood into more wholeness, love and allowance and her need for pointing a finger at a guilty party simply disappeared.

Chapter 6

Releasing Emotional Pain

What is Emotional Pain?

Emotional pain comes in many varieties. A couple in a workshop audience once asked me, "How can we get over the loss of our only child? He was just nineteen." Another lady asked, "How do I get on with my life after my husband walked out?" Still another asked, "How can I go to work every day when I know my boss will be rude and demeaning?"

In this chapter we'll explore the answers. There are myriad ways through such feelings. As with physical pain, the intensity may feel like a small scratch or a gaping wound. Feeling skipped over for our turn in a game is a lot less wounding than the deep emotional scarring of sexual abuse or the death of a loved one.

Emotional pain can be overwhelming. We ask how can we stop hanging on to the hurt? What can we do to shift out of depression, fear, hopelessness, anger, rejection and pain, death and destruction? Can we ever be happy again? How can we change what we feel and get past our walls of resistance? How can we handle emotions without being crushed by them? How can we be free to feel joy again? Emotional pain, kept alive and uncleared, can be an immensely destructive force.

Blocking Pain Stops the Natural Flow

Focusing on and drowning in emotional pain blocks our ability to receive guidance, to connect with our higher self. Once blocked, as with turning a faucet off, nothing comes through. The flow ceases and we feel abandoned by our guides. We believe we've been forgotten, judged, forsaken, and chastised. We feel trapped in our pain but it is our disconnection from our gut feelings that we interpret as pain. Much of this stems from guilt in believing we deserve the pain we feel. Worse, we may criticize ourselves, feeling that we're wallowing in it and should have gotten over it by now. Feelings are not an intellectual process. They don't have to make sense. They just are. We need not judge or avoid emotional pain in ourselves or others. Our highest work is in allowing and moving through the process instead of building walls and constructing detours around our wounds.

Problems in Feeling Pain

Part of the difficulty of allowing ourselves to feel grief, anger, guilt or any so called negative feeling, is that we are performing more than one job during the experience:

- We hold the 'space' for it to happen. This means we create the time and place, even if it's just in our thoughts, for such a focus to occur. This redirects some of our energy away from being able to feel.

- We hang on to a lifeline that will pull us back from the edge of the gulf of feelings.
- We let part of ourselves feel.
- We become a guardian, advising, "Not too far, come back, that's enough."

These all divert us from the pure experience of feeling. In essence, we divide our energies because of our terror of drowning. If you need help to stay focused on your feelings, ask someone to be with you, a close friend or a counselor, to hold the space for you. Get someone to help play the parts. Give yourself the freedom and safety to just feel. You won't drown.

The great fear of drowning and never resurfacing from the depths of the feeling created by the wall of resistance we've built is what makes the feeling more than it is. We have given away our own power to this huge monster and now stand before it, totally disempowered and overwhelmed. We wonder who will rescue us. When we were children and feared the monster under the bed, it was our minds that produced the fear and gave it strength, weight and life itself. Our fears actually empowered that invisible terror. The same is true with our fear of being lost in our emotions, even as adults.

Raphael was stunned when his seemingly perfect life collapsed around him. He was a pillar of the community, an expert in his field, married to a beautiful professional woman and had all the pleasures that wealth could bring. In one short week, his wife informed him that she was having an affair and wanted a divorce and he learned that his job had been extinguished. He went into a two-year cycle of disbelief, followed by anger and then depression. He let himself explore the depths of his feelings without trying to stop himself. In doing so, he learned to allow the process, to breathe through it, to just be present in each moment and to let that moment be okay. He would ask himself, 1) What is happening right now?" and 2) "Can I BE with it?"

As he applied this process, he learned to let each situation be okay and eventually, after months in his despair, his slow acceptance of each moment brought him to an awakening and an extraordinary peace. He had not resisted his own healing. (For more, read his book, *Unconditional Bliss: Finding Happiness in the Face of Hardship* by Raphael Cushnir.

We often hold on so tightly to our lifelines that our feelings are abandoned. Be aware, however, that bridging the gap that exists between thinking and feeling may involve a journey into depression and out the other side into joy.

A List of Emotions

Most of my life I felt emotions were to be hidden behind closed doors. In public, they were to be endured. Around age 10, I hit on the notion of counting things, anything I could see, in order to control my feelings. In other words, I shifted my focus into left-brain, analytical activity. I had stumbled upon a great truth: if I stayed in my thinking self, my left-brain, I could endure emotions. I could think them through, or use my head to cover up the fact that I was feeling anything. I suddenly felt smarter and superior. I didn't have to deal with all those nasty, gluey, little emotions that less intelligent, less disciplined, less restrained people experienced. I had found a way out. They hadn't. Little did I know that I was imprisoning myself. My only gauge had been my family. I didn't know that people in the rest of the world could show their feelings and survive the experience. There was so much about feelings I didn't yet know.

I remember the day a friend asked me, "What are your feelings about that?" I could only come up with a choice of four words— anger, love, hate and joy—and none of those seemed to fit the situation. In a sudden flash, I realized that I had no emotional vocabulary and that therefore my concept of emotion was tremendously limited. So we began to list emotions and I was startled.

What I had been unaware of was that the words explaining how I felt about something were just adjectives. That meant every adjective in the dictionary described and could be attached to a feeling! My concept of emotions was revolutionized. There was a whole world of emotions that I never even knew existed and it had just opened up to me. There was so much more to the feelings game. I had been clueless. Now I felt unlimited. I had an infinite variety of expressions about how I felt and words to describe my reactions to things. It was a doorway for me to experience feelings in safety. In other words, they weren't repulsive and gluey emotions that I had to shut down, but just descriptive adjectives. Here is only a partial listing of those words, but it shows the amazing variety and range our feelings can take:

> *angry, afraid, concerned, distressed, annoyed, agitated, anxious,*
> *irritated, reluctant, reticent, depressed, overwhelmed, moody,*
> *fascinated, intrigued, stimulated, reserved, loving, playful, hopeful,*
> *anticipatory, happy, clear, light, responsive, reactive, detached,*
> *displeased, hateful, jealous, nervous, anxious, restless, drained,*
> *emotionally starved, sorry, remorseful, hostile, humble, exhilarated.*

I have discovered many more to add to my list. I no longer look at my feelings in such a limited way. This discovery gave me permission to be more of who I am, more feeling and more aware. I was no longer lost about how I felt. Not being able to express a feeling in words had been confusing to me, so I ignored my feelings. Now I do not.

Why Bother to Clear Emotional Pain?

Many people do not clear their pain. It serves them somehow. There is a payoff. It may be that they no longer have to strive so hard at achieving a goal, or a promotion. They are excused because of the pain they suffer. Make no mistake, they are suffering. The emotional pain is real. It is just that they can use this newfound experience for a different purpose that only becomes obvious when they are in the midst of the process.

Oftentimes deep emotional pain elicits sympathy and, at the very least, attention. They may have craved this attention for a lifetime and, now that the overwhelming craving is being fed, they are unwilling and perhaps unable to let go of the force that drives it—pain and suffering.

This may not make intellectual sense but, by becoming aware of what we're doing, how we're creating and the unconscious needs that drive us, we can choose to either continue or change. We create our experiences using our emotional selves coupled with our thoughts. It is our emotions that are the operating systems of our lives. They are the underlying creative factors in the personal joy we experience or the personal hell in which we live. In receiving positive reinforcement for our pain, we make victims of ourselves.

Our conscious mind would tell us that we are behaving in a socially unacceptable manner. We don't want that, so we conduct our lives as if diligently attempting to resolve our pain. As long as we think we are doing something, anything, we trick our selves into believing we are progressing towards a solution. In truth, we are simply thrashing around. In a way though, we are trying, very hard, but the conscious mind isn't running the show. The real person in charge, the big kahuna, is the little child who never felt included, approved of, or accepted. She still hurts and our lives become an attempt to rescue her. So again we are playing all three parts of the fear triangle: Victim, Persecutor and Rescuer. But we can wake up.

Accessing Self-Help Guidance

Clearing your emotional state also applies to self-counseling and accessing information for your own use. For instance, if you have low self-worth, as you are receiving intuitive information for yourself, you may use it to criticize yourself. You'll beat yourself up with the information. You then become a victim of your source of advice, be it yourself, your higher self, or guides. These higher aspects of you do not victimize you. Higher guidance never says, "No" and never criticizes you. Higher guidance would not interfere with your freedom of choice.

I often hear people say, "My guidance told me not to go there." Or, "My guidance told me I have to change jobs." These comments are merely our interpretation of guidance's urging. Like a beloved, unconditional lover, it suggests and gently redirects our focus. It leads, guides, suggests, urges, recommends, supports, highlights and offers. It loves. It does not censure, punish, rebuke, shame, blame, reprimand, condemn, lay guilt trips or shut off the faucet stream of connection. It does not make demands, should's, should not's or requirements. Only we do. We interpret and close down because of our fears and self-doubts. Guidance provides useful and repetitive information to gently and constantly remind us of our highest and best path.

Transmutation: The Art of Converting Your Fears into Love

Transmutation is the act of changing a thing into something else. On its grandest level, it is an alchemical process. As with the alchemist of old changing lead into gold, the real objective is to change the perspective of unawake, limited, separate, unworthy human beings into those who know they are unlimited, conscious, connected, wholly worthy, and aspects of God, Creator, All That Is, Source, Oneness. The process we are discussing here is changing our fear-based selves, attached to emotional pain, into beings that release pain naturally and consciously.

This is our highest path to joy. We will always know when we are on that path because of the many signposts of joy along the way. This path may flow through the process of transmutation. We can then use this process by applying it to everyday life occurrences. In doing so, we release our limited human selves to experience our greater spiritual selves. We become more of who we really are—the expression of God experiencing reality as our Self. We become creators of our lives. We leave victimhood behind forever. Love is our natural state. Joy is our nature. Love and Joy are the two highest vibrations we can achieve in the body.

In this process of viewing a fear-based reality through the triads, we become more aware of why we find ourselves in any given situation. The transmutation process further described in Chapter 7, Ten Ways to Choose Joy, will result in raising our personal vibrations and shifting us out of fear. This leads us to clarity in all our experiences, whether spiritual, emotional, intellectual, business or personal.

Remember to begin by asking, "Why did I create this experience in my reality?" rather than, "Why is this happening to me?" The first question is from a self-empowered, conscious being; the second is from a powerless, unconscious victim.

A Constant Process

Shifting our lives into a joy-filled experience is not done by an intellectual decision. It may start there but it needs constant attention, consistent choice, and passion. A desire is awakened to be aware of who you are and who you choose to be in any moment. It is a process. As with losing weight, it may begin with a decision but it is a life choice, a focus, a passion, an application of conscious awareness and attention, consistency and reinforcement all along the way. So, too, does personal transformation require passion, consistency, focus and attention.

When my world was crashing all around me, my decision to ask why I created the financial nightmare was a great step towards healing. It put me in the creator's seat and gave me a self-empowered perspective. My whole thinking process shifted into creating a new reality I much preferred and away from feeling like a victim.

In the beginning, we question each step. "Why? How? What does this mean?" We can't seem to understand something that happens or its purpose in our growth process. That's okay; it's a natural part of learning a new habit and working through a process. We are learning the habit of self-empowerment. When we have the tools to see how and why we create our life as we do, we will have the tools to create our lives as we prefer. Isn't that exciting enough? Read it again!

We will have the tools to create our life exactly as we want it to be because we will KNOW whatever is going on outside us is a reflection of what is within.

We will know how to change what's going on inside, and so our world will shift. This process isn't about changing others. It's about changing our internal programming so that what we magnetize to ourselves is different. It is what we prefer. We choose it. It's not imposed on us. We are in full control. It is by our bidding, our passion, our preference. We can never be victims again.

During the process, we will experience incredible feelings of empowerment. The flower of self unfolds. Stomach knots untangle. Life feels fresher. Over and over again, each time we consciously work through the process, we will feel less and less impotent and more and more energized. When finally the process becomes second nature, we will have created a truly healthy path for our emotions.

Four-Step Process of Transmutation

I first came across this method through a wonderful teacher named Jani King. Since then I have used it over and over to move past stuck points in my thinking process. I also find it an incredibly useful tool in moving through emotional overload.

The four steps of transmutation are:

1) Acknowledge that you created your situation in order to find the pearl of wisdom in it.

2) Acknowledge that all experiences are divine by virtue of their very existence.

3) Do not judge the situation, the process or yourself.

4) Feel the emotions. Feel them in your gut, don't just think them in your head.

Step 1. Discovering the Pearl of Wisdom

Recognize that there is a pearl of wisdom in the experience you have created. Seek it out. Look for the payoff, the key to how this serves you. Remove the concepts of guilt, blame and criticism.

I remember an incident with my psychic friend, Karen, at a restaurant. One of the men at our table, Rick, said he had chronic knee pain and it was hurting a lot. Although he didn't ask, she offered to heal him. She stood up and began a high-pitched and very loud vocal toning in the middle of the restaurant. All the diners stopped and stared, stunned by her performance. I felt this was grandstanding and didn't see the need for it. My reaction was total embarrassment and I wanted to crawl under the table.

I began to intellectualize my feelings and explain to the other people at our table what Karen was doing. They had never even met psychics before and were already unsure about it all. I began telling them that this was an ancient form of healing and the tones created vibrations, etc, etc. The result of her toning, which went on and on, was that Rick's knee was greatly improved and later we learned that it never bothered him again.

I wondered why I had created this experience. What was the gem in awareness that would help me uncover myself and see my own fears? How could I use this situation and its emotional impact to learn about me and grow past the fear associated with it?

Discovering this pearl took a long time and, as it turned out, there were actually several. First, I had to deal with my embarrassment. Every time I thought about the incident, I became embarrassed all over again. So why was I embarrassed? I knew Karen hadn't "made" me feel anything. Remember, anytime we react to, deny, or defend something, we have an issue with it; and it's *our* issue! I knew I had a big one here. After a few days, I began uncovering some of those many issues.

For one, I saw how important it was that I be seen in a positive light by these people. In other words, I allowed my self-worth to be determined outside of me, giving away my power to strangers. Another was my discovery that I felt Karen should not conduct herself this way, but in a manner that would meet my expectations. I was expecting her to give her power away to me to determine how she should behave. My reaction had been so intense that I knew there was a gem in here for me. Finally I realized that I had tried to suppress my very powerful feelings of humiliation and had gone straight to intellectualizing to cover them up. I was still afraid to feel openly.

By staying out of self-criticism and allowing information to percolate up through my feelings and thinking, I found the insights in the experience.

Step 2. Connect with Your Own Divinity by Knowing that All Feelings Are Equally Divine

All creation is divine because it comes from Source, Creator, Isness, God. This includes all the feelings you've ever had or could have, good or not. Any so called negative emotion such as anger, jealousy or greed is also divine. Unwanted emotions are just shadow aspects of the Self that we have not yet loved. Their very existence proves their divinity. Spirit created it and Spirit is divine. Thus *everything* is divine, including what our human and limited perspectives have judged as bad. Allow everything to have a positive side and you will be able to shift your perspective. Let go of your criticism. Let go of your judgment. Simply embrace everything as perfect just as it is and divine in its essence. Allow it all.

When we align with this knowing, we release all our hostility toward the negative emotional experience. It is incorporated into our higher vibration and is dissipated. Our search for something positive in an emotionally charged situation leads us to a higher vibration and neutralizes the sting of the "bad" feeling. Seeking the hidden wisdom in a situation and raising our consciousness to align with its deepest wisdom results in seeing the divinity of the experience. We open up to the grander part of the Self and attract the very answers we seek.

As with most of us, I'd been taught that anger is unacceptable and unladylike. It means you're out of control, which translates into unlovable. Anger is an offense punishable by reprimand, shunning, dirty looks, shaming, silent treatment, humiliation and worse, GUILT.. In my family, we quickly learned to bury anger. But it still eats away, submerged, waiting to surface unbidden and explosively. Here's what happened to me when I learned that all feelings are valid and divine, including anger.

I was returning from out of town after visiting my mother, who today holds me on a pedestal after years of hatred. (That same hate is now directed towards another sister.) Mother lives in a world of replay of injustices received and perceived. Because she constantly thinks of them and has few others to vent this anger on, she filled our conversations from sunup to bedtime with stories of treachery and victimization, told and retold, each time creatively augmented. After only one day of this, I was resentful and angry at not being able to be heard. I often said, "Please let's not spend time talking about it. Let's change the subject. You've told me all this before." But she played the same old tapes over and over, mixing facts to form a picture of my sister as Snidely Whiplash.

Having had my fill, I left the visit with Mother early, glad to be on my way home. At the airport, I returned the rental car. The clerk was cold and defensive as she told me that I'd exceeded the 24-hour limit by one hour. To my amazement, this meant that I had to pay for a second day, doubling the cost. I was mad and, the madder I became, the more deaf she became. She reminded me of the telephone operator receiving an emergency call and saying, "I'm sorry, pu-lease put in a-nother dieum." You know you're just talking to a robot with no desire to feel anything. Even if she had said, "I'm very sorry it wasn't explained to you, but it's our policy," I would have felt better. But she wouldn't acknowledge me or my feelings. I wanted to say many things to her, none of them pleasant.

Then I saw her nametag. In my psychic work, I use names as a doorway to access information about a person. Based on thousands of readings, her name was one that invariably meant she'd been sexually molested as a child. Then I realized that her hair and appearance were de-feminized, with no leeway for her female side, as if that would be too vulnerable, too revealing, or might lead to being abused again. Her only femaleness was the uniform she wore for the rental agency. Without it, I could visualize her in baggy pants and tee shirt as her home "uniform."

I was torn between feeling compassion for her and being angry. I realized that she was simply reacting to my emotions with emotional shutdown of her own. Her past had taught her that there was probably no safe way for her to deal with someone else's feelings, so just block them out. I'm sure she never intended to hurt or insult me, and never thought (or cared about) what her actions might arouse in me. She only knew fear and reacted like a frightened animal.

Then I realized I had a choice. I could say something but was so angry that I could only accuse and blame, and I can't do that when I'm conscious of it. So I took a step back and asked myself why I had created this experience. Then I realized that this situation was an outpicturing of my unexpressed anger at my mother, coupled with the frustration of not being able to find an open restaurant on the way to the airport due to a holiday.

In that moment, I took responsibility for my creation and faced the next choice. I asked myself "Dolly, how do you want to feel in the next now? Do you want to carry your anger around with you? How would it serve you to continue to be angry?"

I paid the rental car bill and chose to drop the anger, but still wasn't sure how to make the shift come about. I found a restaurant in the terminal but they had nothing I really wanted. When the manager was kind enough to offer to make a cheese sandwich, I agreed. While paying in advance, I was aware that I was still carrying some anger and was sure to create another event to allow me to be mad again, and that this situation was probably it. But how?

I asked the manager, "What kind of bread will you use?"

He pointed to a thick huge sourdough thing. Yuk, I thought. I'd have been really upset with that, so I canceled the order.

I wandered the terminal, hoping another food source was available, letting go of some of my anger as I walked. I successfully passed the ice cream stand, which would have been an old pattern to "fix" mad, pleased I'd passed that test. Then I came on a small sandwich counter and found a tuna salad sandwich. Perfect, well almost. The bread was double-thick but I was letting go of the anger a little more.

I paid for the sandwich and debated where to sit. At an empty table, I could have sat alone and hung on to my mad, while mentally and emotionally reliving my recent injuries. However, another woman sat alone so I asked her if I might join her. She readily accepted my self-invitation and I watched my conversation, the gradual ebb of anger, and the final choosing of joy as I told funny stories and then jokes. When I began laughing, I knew I'd finally shifted my anger. What a job it had been but I was glad I'd consciously decided to move in that direction. Having consciously gone through that lengthy method the first time, I thought, it will be easier and faster the next time.

Today, I love my anger and that of others around me—well, perhaps not completely yet, but it's not as scary as before and I'm beginning to feel differently about it.

Rajni, my first teacher said, "You can choose joy. It is always a choice."

And so it is.

Step 3. Do Not Judge the Process

Judgment stops the flow. What we judge is what we do not yet love about ourselves. Ultimately, everything is about us, especially what we judge. Judgment throws an internal switch telling the self-protective ego to stop the allowing process. It decides to make this decision in spite of not knowing future events that will have a direct bearing on future perceptions. In other words, it says, "I refuse to look at this event from a higher perspective. I choose not to see the grander vision that could show me why this event took place."

For instance, we get a flat tire and begin judging our mate or mechanic for not replacing it when it was obviously balding. Instead of judgment, we might expand our view of things to allow for our having been delayed so we could meet someone or avoid a driving problem ahead. Stopping the process by judging it is a waste of time and energy.

Step 4. Feel the Feeling in Your Gut, Not Your Head. Allow the Experience

The next part of this process of transforming unwanted emotions is a challenge to those of us who have been taught that feelings are nasty, sticky things that trap us like quicksand, suck us in and overwhelm us. You may also have been taught that feelings are unacceptable, and been ridiculed for them. You may have been validated only for thinking through an emotional situation instead of feeling through it. Our teachers, parents and clergy were often at a loss to understand or cope with others' feelings, let alone their own. They redirected us away from our gut where we could feel it, and into our heads to think it through.

Set your thinking aside and let yourself become sensitive to where you feel a feeling in your body. It may be in your shoulders, your knees, your lower back, or your gut. Each one tells you a different story about how this feeling is affecting you. For example, if you feel a tensing, a weightiness or oppression in your shoulders, perhaps you are shouldering too much in the drama you're in. If it's in your legs, perhaps you're having difficulty in taking the next step and making a move forward in your life.

When you consciously begin to allow yourself to feel the feelings, you will begin to notice that your vocabulary changes. Likewise, if you would pay attention to your vocabulary, you would see how you are relating to your world and can change it by changing the verb "I think" to "I feel."

Begin to pay attention to your responses, those of others and to questions about feelings. For example, suppose you are asked, "How do you feel about your mother?" You might reply, "Well, I think she's pretty." You just countered a feeling question with a thinking answer. In other words, you intellectualized the feeling and skipped right over it. You responded with how you *think*. A feeling answer might be, "She feels nurturing, loving, over-protective, demanding or a little crazy." Watch for this and you'll begin to see how you handle your feelings. Do you think them through, or do you connect with them and feel into them?

One day I was driving back from a huge psychic expo. I had just experienced an emotional three-day-long dark night of the soul, an intense upheaval that resulted in a personal transformation of the way I viewed and experienced life. (Many spiritual transformations that are super-charged with feelings take three to three and a half days to pass through, during which you realign your body, mind and spirit to a new vibration.)

After climbing out of my emotional pit, I realized that my life had changed. I began using only "I feel" statements. I had finally become a feeler, not just a thinker. I had been so overwhelmed and had connected so strongly with my feelings that I'd been transformed. It was now okay for me to feel. In fact, it was a lot more than okay. I couldn't experience my surroundings and my self in any other way. I wanted to feel. I *wanted* to get caught up in the sensations. I could not conceive of my life without knowing it through my senses. Life no longer made sense without my feelings. I had been locked in my head for so long, fearing drowning in my feelings and getting lost. I had only been lost in my head, a mind trap that separated me from the most authentic part of my life.

So, disconnect from your head and let yourself feel. Stop the thinking process. Stop analyzing things. Stop categorizing experiences. But how do you avoid drowning in those feelings once you've allowed them to be awakened and addressed? One way is to literally set a timer for perhaps 5, 10 or 20 minutes when you feel yourself going into a feeling that you may not prefer. Then go fully into it for that period. Allow the onslaught of emotion. Recall the times when you had the same feeling. Jump into the ocean of your feelings until the buzzer sounds. Visualize yourself swimming, seeing your feelings as companion swimmers. What beings are there with you? Dolphins, sharks, colored fish, unknown shapes? When you delve into a feeling, it loses its power over you. You come out on the other side of the set time period feeling as if you had made new friends with those feelings. At the very least, you have torn down the walls of defense against those emotions and thus discharged their power. What you resist persists. What you love is transmuted.

Use this process every day to train yourself how to shift your emotions. As you create this new habit, you begin to shift to a more centered state and begin to see the larger perspective on events as they happen. You become less reactive and more balanced. This simple process will become an ever-present tool in your transmuting fear to love.

Next we will look at concrete ways to achieve and remain in a state of Love.

Chapter 7

Ten Ways to Choose Joy, or Moving out of Fear and into Love

1. Make a Joy List

As we begin this journey of changing from the Fear triangle to the Love triangle, here is an easy first step. Create a Joy List. This is so incredibly simple that you may think it's too silly to do, but it's one of those life-changing things that is incredibly effective. Get a lovely notebook. This is going to be a long list, maybe 300 - 400 items or more. For the first five minutes of each waking hour, focus on what brings you joy and write it all down. No have tos or shoulds. No limits on whether practical or not; on possible or probable. Just dream away about what is, what you have, what may be and what you'd love. Duplications on your list are just fine.

This little exercise establishes a pattern of allowing yourself to focus on joy. Remember, the emotional energy you focus on brings you more of the same. How hard can this decision be? Only as hard as you make it. As fearsome as owning that you create your life. You will be setting out on a path of joy, in a real way, beginning to consciously create it. Is it not totally reasonable to begin your journey to light, love and joy by beginning to focus on it? Take time now and begin writing your joy list.

Linda had a very short joy list that read:

I love to take long baths

I love to go deep-sea fishing.

I love to spend time with my son.

When she looked at this list, really looked at it, she realized that her 22-year-old son lived 200 miles away; that she lived hours from the ocean and that her home only had a shower in it. No wonder she had a hard time finding happiness in her life. She changed her residence to include a tub, scheduled more time with her son, planned fishing trips and then added more things to her joy list.

When you are feeling anything other than what you prefer to feel, go do something on that list. Pet a puppy, walk barefoot in the grass, take a ferryboat ride, stroll through a park, chat with the first person you see, sit down and take a break, read a book, or compliment someone. You are thus consciously creating joy in your life and choosing to act on it This is how you create what you'd prefer… every single time.

My friend, Jim, once made his Joy List and listed 9 things:

God

Wife

Children

Family

Religion

Music

Job

Horses

Friends

I remarked, "No wonder you're not happy."

He adamantly replied, "Of course I'm happy. What makes you think I'm not?"

"Well," I said, "because you've left off the most important thing."

He responded, "Not only have I not left anything off, I wouldn't even change their order of priority. What do you think I left off?"

I pointed out, "You've left yourself off your list."

He thought a moment and retorted, quite indignantly, "All those things on my list are me."

"They are not you," I replied. "They are all outside of you."

"I can't be on my own Joy list. Putting myself on it would be selfish," Jim complained.

"No," I replied," that would be centered in Self. It's the opposite of being self-centered. Self-centered is ego-based. Centered in Self is spirit-based. It is finding the still small voice within, becoming silent and listening. Being centered in Self is knowing you are the source of your own joy and sadness, as well as of all your feelings."

I let that sink in and then asked, "What would happen if all those things on your joy list were suddenly gone from your life? Who would you be and how would you be happy then?

"Hmm," he replied. "I'd have to think about that."

Seven months later, his church, his family and his friends had all been ripped from him. To phrase it more accurately, he had created the experience of detachment from all those things that had represented joy yet were outside of him. Little by little, Jim began to learn that he was the creator of his reality. He had to learn how to love himself. He realized that if he continued to look to all he'd lost for his happiness, he would become a powerless victim. He would be giving away responsibility to others for creating joy in his life. He began to see how dis-empowering this was. He saw how addicted he was to all the things on his Joy list and how they had been a lifeline for him. He began to see that he was a creator and that the true source of all his joy must come from within. He saw how co-dependent he was on all those external things. He began waking up and taking conscious responsibility for creating his whole life. Today Jim acknowledges that he is the creator of his experiences and he is walking in joy.

So much of the time, we have no clue as to what things bring us joy. Certainly all these things are outside of us so don't look to them for happiness. Happiness comes from within, from the attitude and feelings we bring to those things on our list. The Joy List exercise not only helps us begin to focus on joy regularly but it also gives us a handy reference list of things to do when we aren't feeling happy. So often when we're feeling down, we pout, withdraw or become shut down. With this joy list, we can go do something on it and already be certain that it will assist us in feeling joyful again.

2. *What We Focus On, We Get More Of*

This is the Law of Attraction, which I first became aware of in an Abraham tape by Esther Hicks. As noted earlier, we are always creating our reality by what we think and how we tie emotions to those thoughts. If we constantly tell ourself, "I can't afford it," or we worry about, "I don't have enough money for the rent," or we believe, "I'll never find anyone who'll love me," the energy we project actually creates these things in our world so we don't have enough money, or we can't afford that suit or Mr. or Ms. Right doesn't come along. But when we realize we are magnificent and powerful creators who put forth so much energy in the form of fear that it created our existence, then we can own the fact that we can now create a different existence. We can create the one we want.

Begin the process by monitoring your thoughts and feelings. Pay attention to them. Note them, but don't judge them. Simply be aware of them. Above all, have those feelings. Then ask yourself, "Is this what I want to think and feel? Is this what I'd like to continue to expend my energies in creating?" If not, then decide what you prefer, what you would actually like to have in your reality instead: joy, love, money, health, a relationship, peace or abundance? If so, then focus on what you prefer—abundance rather than the lack of money; health instead of fearing cancer or heart problems; love instead of fearing rejection or abandonment. You can shift your focus. It takes only 17 seconds of focusing with your thoughts and feelings on a particular thing, and your personal magnetic field changes. You bring up the feeling of what you prefer to have in your world. Stay in that feeling for 17 seconds. Your energy begins to shift. Your body begins putting out different electrical signals into your auric field, the field that surrounds the body. The longer you stay in the feeling, the more magnetic to it you become. Should you stay in the feeling of joy, then you begin attracting more joy to you. You literally magnetize feelings and experiences that bring joy to you. Your world begins to shift.

We are already using this law of attraction to create our reality, although unconsciously. And since it creates according to the programming of our subconscious emotions, we are usually creating precisely what we do not want.

We expend so much energy on the fear of things. Worry begets worry. Fear begets fear. The universe doesn't care what we choose. It is non-judgmental. It simply brings us more of what we focus on. If it's fear, then guess what? We get more fear. So decide how you'd like your world to look, then begin focusing on it, and FEEEEEEL it! Remember, love begets love. Joy begets joy.

Steve had become such a victim that, in the midst of his personal crisis, everyone else became his persecutor. He was so focused on feeling attacked by everyone and everything that he managed to create some amazing quirks of self-destruction. They were such impossible situations that, if they had been positive outcomes, they would have been deemed miracles.

For instance, he had a small government disability pension from his military days. Such supplements are usually inviolable. After his wife left him, he fell behind in the mortgage payments and his home was repossessed. Then he had a heart attack. His sister helped him move his belongings into storage and then stole them for drug money. To top it all off, his government stipend, his only source of income, was retracted in a bizarre ninety-day window of policy change. "Miracles" such as these are the result of intense negative focus. Imagine what Steve could have done if he'd used that same intensity of focus to consciously create joy and love instead of fear and victimhood.

3. Begin Appreciating Something, Anything

When you decide you've had enough of an undesirable feeling, you can begin to shift immediately by changing your focus to appreciating something, anything. Appreciate one thing, anything, then more things, until all you feel is the vibration of appreciation.

Find things you can be thankful for. Begin with one thing close to you and then expand it to your home, city, country or world. Perhaps you could begin by listing the color of your hair, your manicure, the cozy fire in the fireplace, your smooth skin, the terry cloth robe, the silk in your tie, the cool breeze on your face, or the aroma of fresh-baked cherry pie. As you begin with one thing, it is the barest of lifelines. As you add more to it, it becomes a string, then a rope, thicker and thicker until it is a humongous, gigantic, armload of "feel goods." And since the Universe knows that you're focusing on all the good things in your life, guess what? *You get more!*

Pretty soon, you're standing over here feeling good, instead of over there feeling bad. You're standing in the middle of feeling appreciation. And guess what? It's a great feeling, so uplifting. It's a much higher vibration than anger or depression or fear. How it works seems almost magical.

You have moved through an aspect of yourself, a shadow part of you. It's always you standing in your own way, even when it looks like someone else. From this new happier perspective, you have a basis to consciously create what you'd prefer to see happen. Remember it only takes 17 seconds in an emotional focus to begin your shift.

START NOW!

Exercise: Find one thing to appreciate NOW! Then find another. And another. Feel the appreciation happening.

4. Love An Unwanted Feeling To Death

When you are hurting and finally decide you've had enough, you can love the pain to death. Once you make the determination to be done with the pain, you can use any method possible to shift your awareness into one of love. It may be music, poetry, spiritual books, walking, meditating with nature, or journaling. By shifting your focus, you allow yourself to move into an altered state, altered from the downward spiral you were in. You literally step into a clear space in which *you choose your next feeling*. You are now most vulnerable to the experiences of love and joy. Your vibrations are elevated. Your emotions are in an open place and available to you. In this state, choose love. Breathe it up from within the depths of you. Allow memories of loving experiences and events to bubble up to your consciousness. Revel in them. Swim in them. Allow yourself to re-experience them until you *are* the experience of love. Then you will know *you* are the source of Love, not something outside of you.

Now, while in this loving space, bring forth the situation that has triggered you to throw your emotions off-center. Wrap this event in the warm embrace of Love, the love you are, the love you have regenerated within through memory and feelings. Literally, love it to death. This is what it means when poets write, "Love conquers all," so, *be* it.

The Power of Love to Heal

Love can cure. Since it is the highest vibration possible, when it exists unconditionally, it has the ability to heal physically and emotionally. Miraculous healings occur when love, often in the form of prayers, surrounds a person. When that person raises his own vibrations to match those of the love and prayer around him, he aligns with them, absorbs them into his body and heals in the twinkling of an eye. Emotional healing responds in exactly the same way. In both cases, we are the source of the healing because we choose to align with those prayers and love. No one heals us. We step up our vibrations and align with the higher vibration of wholeness. Doctors and holy men provide the trigger by reminding us of that higher vibration. They are the instruments by which we activate our cure. Remember, we are not at anyone's mercy, for cure or for harm. We are creators. Thus we can never be victims of someone's fixing us or not fixing us. No matter what our condition, we are not broken. We have created our reality.

We use the vibrations set up by others through prayer or medicine, and accept them and align with them. We are powerful in our curative ability. Our emotional health is as important as our physical health.

Here is one situation in which the power of love healed gut-wrenching fear. My partner faced a great threat and I was in fear. Not just a little worry, but the, "Oh my God!" kind where you stop eating in mid-bite because your throat closes, the pit of your stomach becomes a hard knot and you freeze. He was on probation from one of those incredible run-ins with the court system where you are convicted and imprisoned, though innocent. There was still one year to go and all his actions were scrutinized. He had played the victim in his life for many years and this was one of the consequences. His life had turned around but he was playing out the balance of the scenario with the one year remaining. Given sufficient cause, the court system could re-incarcerate him but, despite this looming threat, we rarely gave any energy or space in our reality to fear.

One day, while jogging alone, he encountered a group of nine- and ten-year-old children waiting for a school bus. A young boy was mercilessly kicking a little girl, who was screaming and pleading for him to stop. On seeing my partner, she asked for his help. He immediately pulled the boy off the girl, saying, "If you want someone to pick on, beat me up."

The incident was over, the bus arrived and he continued jogging. The next day, while jogging again, a policeman stopped him and accused him of abusing the boy. He was stunned.

He tried to explain the situation to the policeman, suggesting he speak to the children who witnessed the event and were there again waiting for the bus. The policeman was antagonistic, fear-based and showed it, judging and condemning. He took my partner's name and particulars before letting him go to finish his jogging route. When my partner got home, he told me what happened. I caught his fear and bought it and owned it, lock, stock and barrel. I felt re-imprisonment was a real threat and fear raged through each cell of my body. My mind raced ahead with "what ifs." I was scared through and through. I knew the principles to overcome fear and how to deal with it but I was still locked in the paralysis of the emotion.

I began work on myself as I knew I could not change my partner, only myself, and one of us had to get healthy. I began reading uplifting books, listening to uplifting music and TV programs and did some meditating and journaling. I did whatever it took to shift my focus away from fear. I began by asking why we had created this experience and concluded it was to overcome the fear of his vulnerability, and to deal with his issues relating to being a hurt little boy just like the abusive and hurting little bully in this story. It was also about healing issues having to do with false accusation. It was a tough challenge. Even in the midst of my fear, I knew there were worse trials but it didn't make my pain any less real.

I remembered from *"A Course in Miracles"* the lesson that says, "Your attack thoughts attack your invulnerability." I was reminded that from my higher perspective, I was invulnerable, which comforted me. Each thought, prayer and meditation helped move me into higher awareness and out of the lower vibration of fear.

That night, I couldn't go to sleep. I sat up watching the late movie, *Goodbye Charlie*, a love story about a man who was a terrible womanizer. He died but received a second chance to redeem himself by coming back to earth in a woman's body in order to find just one woman who really loved him. In his new woman's body, he was date-raped by his old buddy who now found his sexy female body irresistible. After nine months, he/she delivered a baby girl. When her baby was placed on her breast, he/she experienced unconditional love, and having found a female who loved him/her, died, redeemed.

It was so full of love that I was in tears. Being so vulnerable, I was open to my feelings and felt the enormity of the love shared in that last moment of the mother's life and the first moment of her child's. I allowed the loving feeling to manifest to its fullest extent in my body. Into that now-altered state, I intentionally brought my fears and allowed them to rest there, cradled. Since I was in such a loving space, the love I felt embraced my fear and it was gone, dissolved and absorbed into the greater emotion. I was healed. I had "loved my pain to death" and knew it was gone. I was so overwhelmed.

In that moment, I knew I could finally rest, and went up to bed. My partner was fast asleep, so I woke him to share this experience. He immediately went into guilt and self-recrimination over causing me pain and hurting me by entangling me in his fears, but again love overwhelmed the fear-based feelings. He could literally feel what was happening and entered the same space of total and unconditional love. Love is contagious.

In that moment, the entire situation was healed. We never heard back from the policeman or the little boy or the parents. The matter evaporated. For the next day and a half, we existed in an altered state, an extraordinary loving, exalted perception. We were both conscious of it and loved and allowed it fully without analysis. It was a real demonstration of the power of love to embrace and heal anything.

Love did not attack the fear, or overcome it, or overpower it. Those words are from our old warrior consciousness. Love does not do battle. Love simply loves. Its vibration is so powerful and all encompassing that no other emotion can exist in its embrace. My terror was embraced in love and dissolved into nothingness.

I carry this knowing with me to take out and look at every now and then. I sit in amazement at the power of unconditional love and and at the fact that any one of us may attain it, even in the depths of gripping fear.

It is a choice.

5. Giving Away What You Need

When you're hurting and in pain, find someone else to whom you can give what you need. When we give away what we need, physically or emotionally, we have recognized at a deep internal level that we already have it within ourselves, or we wouldn't be able to give it away. Following are several illustrations.

There is a lovely story of John, a teenage boy, desperately hurt and in great pain from a car accident that severed his left arm. He was sullen and unresponsive, withdrawing further with each moment. His mother was becoming unable to reach him. In that same hospital ward was a two-year-old, crying incessantly from pain. The crying and intermittent screaming had gone on for three days. One day, John's mother couldn't take it any more so she went over to the two-year-old's bed and picked him up. She brought the screaming boy over to her son and laid him on John's chest. John was stunned but instinctively placed his one good arm upon the boy, connecting in the only way his raw emotions would allow, soothing both of them. The crying ceased; the teenager smiled. Pain-to-pain, heart-to-heart, connection made. Later, the amazed nurse wondered why she'd never thought of it. From that one incident, a special healing program was begun that helped thousands to heal each other. Those who need the gift of healing receive it when they give it away. There are no victims here and no rescuers. It is a grand application of: "Giving is receiving and receiving is giving."

When we have financial problems, if we give money away, such as by leaving a larger tip for the waitress or giving to a street person, we will begin to know wealth. It is the person-to-person connection that makes the difference. Writing a check and sending it to a charity helps, but our hearts open more easily to a heart directly in front of us. When you are lonely, find someone else who is lonely and give of yourself. When you feel unloved, find someone to love: a child, a puppy, a person in a nursing home, a co-worker or a neighbor. What you give away in these circumstances is received in the same moment. Thus the giving is the receiving and the receiving is the giving. You are giving to yourself. You can see there is no real "other." You are one and the same, both aspects of the same All-that-is, the great I AM.

Because of religious differences, Jim was shunned by his family and they refused to allow him to see his adored grandchildren who were the light of his life. Instead of playing the victim role, he decided to "adopt" every child he encountered under the age of five as if they were one of his. In grocery stores, malls and ice cream shops, he connected with each baby and toddler, cooing to them, waving and playing. If they were screaming or throwing a fit, he barked like a dog, asking, "Is that your doggie?"

Hundreds of mothers and fathers out there are grateful for the bearded stranger who cared enough to "woof." He was interrupting the pattern of an unhappy child, silencing the screams and relieving frayed nerves. The neighborhood's toddlers were lavished with attention, play and the gift of a few tee shirts and toys now and then. There was always the ready wave hello and good-bye, the missing thumb act, disappearing coin tricks, and the barking doggie. This wonderful man learned how to give love to others' children and in doing so, mended his own heart.

6. Create a Wellness Plan

What is a Wellness Plan? In a nutshell, it's a healing plan for all four levels of being. How do we create one?

Physical level: Pay attention to exercise, perhaps just walking or participating in a sport. Be gentle to you. Watch what foods you ingest, listening to what the body needs, not the taste buds. If you can't trust your body knowledge, get the help of a professional until you can. Perhaps follow a mild body cleansing diet, especially at the change of seasons. Drink plenty of water. It cleanses and flushes system-wide.

Emotional level: On an emotional level, honor your feelings by acknowledging and allowing them, not avoiding, restricting and stuffing them.

Mental level: On a mental level, read self-help books, perhaps get counseling, maybe join a group with others of your same interests or brand new ones. Begin a journal, connecting your thoughts and feelings, compose poetry or write a story, paint a picture or play a musical instrument.

Spiritual level: Meditate, pray, seek spiritual guidance, read uplifting books, listen to music, attend spiritual gatherings.

There are many other aspects to your own personalized Wellness Plan. The point is that each of us chooses our own focus and creates the path that works best for us. After all, your wellness journey is about YOU, no one else.

Why Do I Need a Wellness Plan?

A Wellness Plan allows us to create a balanced life. It addresses balance on all four aspects of the self: Physical, Emotional, Mental and Spiritual. If we are feeling off-balance, out of sorts on any level, it affects our judgment, awareness, self-worth, abilities, attitude and feelings. It certainly affects our ability to approach a feeling in a healthy way or to go through the experience of that feeling without fear of drowning in it. If you are physically ill with a cold, you may treat it with antibiotics, vitamin C, Echinacea or other medicine or herbs. But the real issue of why you got the cold in the first place is not based in the physical body.

When you look at your emotions and thoughts, you will see the real cause of your dis-ease. Most times, colds are caused by congestion in your daily life, that is, feelings left un-addressed, or situations that you responded to in overload, such as too much going on all at once. When you begin to resolve an imbalance on any one of these levels by looking at all four levels, you begin to create a holistic approach to your daily life. Leave one area out of your Wellness Plan, and you leave yourself open to recreating the same dis-ease over and over again. It may not be a cold. It may be getting cheated in business time and time again. It may be having rotten relationships. Each dysfunction can be overcome through introspection and through approaching wellness on all four levels. You are a whole self. You cannot go anywhere or be anywhere that all four parts of you do not go along. How would you expect to resolve imbalance by addressing only one aspect of yourself?

Remember, we are spiritual beings having physical experiences, not physical beings having spiritual experiences.

7. Create a Perfect Day or 365 of Them!

From the power of owning that you are the source of all your feelings comes a wonderful ability to experience life in excited anticipation, more like a little child than an adult. Every moment of every day becomes Christmas when you know something good is coming.

Long before I got serious about metaphysics, I decided to choose a perfect day. Rather, I chose a day that no matter what happened, would be perfect. I decided to create it that way. Something about the idea of making a perfect day was irresistible.

I used to drive from appointment to appointment and wouldn't put the radio on and refused to have a cell phone. That uninterrupted space became an altered space and answers and new ideas, both practical and philosophical, came out of nowhere. This concept entered my head during one of those times. I hadn't yet realized that it was my connection with guidance, my higher self, or whatever one calls it. But it was reliable, insightful, felt good, and the many answers and ideas worked.

The elements of such a day, no matter what would happen, were unbelievably simple. I chose April 21. I *knew*, for example, that even if a policeman stopped me and gave me a ticket, it would be the best experience possible in that now, and a doorway to something wonderful. I'd let myself fantasize about what that wonderful something might be. Maybe the policeman would have stopped me so that I wasn't going to drive into an accident ahead; or he would be a fabulous contact in my business. I *knew* absolutely, unequivocally and totally that, no matter what happened, no matter how it appeared on any other day, on this day it would be fantabulous!

For days prior to the 21st, everyone around me knew it was coming up. I told them all about it. I wanted to share it. It wasn't just for me;

everyone was involved in the joy. I was in great anticipation and excitement, but never expectation of anything that might happen. I just knew that whatever did show up, I was going to perceive it as extra-ordinary, that is, totally out of the ordinary.

Many people joined in my joy and excitement. I made it clear it wasn't a day for presents, just presence. I delighted in telling everyone with whom I did business. It was such a happy choice, and it delighted many others and me. Amazing things happened on those April 21s, and they continue to do so. They weren't such unusual things. On the contrary, they were quite ordinary but were slanted by my perception and viewed in a new light. It didn't matter if it was just buying groceries or pumping gas. There was a joy to experience, to share, to involve others in. This was definitely not about aloneness. It was about at-one-ment with everyone. I connected with everyone from a heart space, from joy. I could have lit up a room with my joy, and it was contagious.

After a couple of years of this, it dawned on me that I could have two days a year like that. So I planned six months down the road and selected October 21. Immediately, I asked, "Why limit it to only two days a year. I could have 365 of them." And so my life became more joy-filled. I created many such experiences. I began living consciously in joy each and every day. I knew that whatever came my way was absolutely perfect and looked for the silver lining everywhere.

The way I related to every little thing changed. The slightest event became charged with excitement and aliveness. I became conscious of the smallest things. Think of it this way. When you sit, feel the chair or sofa or cushion on your bum; feel your feet on the floor, the air on your face; smell the scent of the pages of the book; feel the book cover on your fingertips; see the letters as they make words, paragraphs and pages. Each of these things in itself is a "no-thing" but, taken all together in awareness, they constitute aliveness. Each moment becomes charged with life and presence. All of it is a state of *being*, not doing.

After all, we're *human beings* not *human doings*. We don't have to *do* anything to experience all of this except to pay attention and focus ourself. Every moment becomes rich and full. All of it is already happening. Pay attention and focus your awareness at many points during the day, knowing that whatever happens is a gift you get to open from *your* perspective, whatever kind of joy it is, and that you created it so. Then, every day is just like Christmas.

It's unlikely that you could think like this and still remain a victim. Incidents that would ordinarily have caused a negative reaction become transformed into wondrous experiences. You stop looking for the persecutor; you honor your creative ability and apply it in each moment. You put joy and love into your energy field and attract more of the same.

If we just see the perfection in all things each day, all day long, whether it's the upset grocery clerk or the alcoholic street bum, and if we see them all as God and absolutely perfect just as they are, then we become the instruments of change in this universe. It all happens through us. We are the end of the line and the center for change in the universe. We make the difference in consciousness, because All is One.

Exercise: Create your own perfect day. Choose a date. Look forward to the excitement, the freedom, the non-judgmental quality of this day. You do not have to plan the form. The universe will take care of that. Journal what experiences you have on that day because you brought a focus of joy to it. If you have difficulty doing this, think of yourself as a child getting excited for Christmas, or recall your wedding day, or your first big travel experience.

8. Remove the Label from the Energy

No energy is bad. Simply tear off your label on that energy: unhappy, angry, fearful, guilty, excited, scared or enthusiastic. Underneath, it is just raw energy. You have unlocked it from its prison of judgment and limitation. Use it freely. Apply it in any way that assists you. By your intention, send the energy to heal a sore finger, mend an emotional hurt, empower yourself, charge ahead in business, or try again where you feel you failed. How would you choose to use energy if you had an unlimited supply of it? You do. It's yours for free. You've just judged a lot of it, but no energy is good or bad. It just is. It is how one applies it that makes it appear good or bad. If you plug in a hair dryer and dry your hair, electricity appears to be good. But if you stick your finger into a wall socket and shock yourself, electricity may appear to be bad. Application makes all the difference in the world.

So, too, with energy. Powerful emotions may appear to overwhelm, especially powerful negative emotions. But if you simply tear off the negative label and use that powerful raw energy to boost your healing abilities, or clear your anger, or create a sense of allowance in your moment, you will have acted from the center of your being. Your recognition of emotion as just "energy-in-motion" and your decision to apply that raw energy in a positive way are sure signs of your own spiritual growth.

Looking at Pain Differently

What if we didn't know pain was supposed to be a bad thing? What if we didn't know a feeling was "bad" or that what we were feeling was "pain"? We would experience the feeling differently. We might just notice where in the body this new feeling occurred. We could focus our awareness in the pain and follow the feeling in the body. By doing so, we unblock it. We don't cut the pain off and distance ourselves from it. We merely align with it and experience its flow into dissipation and out of the body. When we smash a finger in a car door, we immediately react by holding our breath, perhaps squeezing the finger in an attempt to separate ourselves from the hurt and shut it off from our body. All these actions stop the flow. No breath. No willingness to feel. Fear of pain. Pain is just an experience to move through. We have choices as to how to do that. We can align with it or not. We align by tearing down our walls of resistance and allowing ourselves to let the feeling exist free of judgment.

For years, Mandy had suffered from terrible headaches. She began to cease resisting the pain and, instead, began to allow it, relax her body and align with the feelings. Instead of increasing, the headaches began to lessen in intensity. As she breathed into the pain, it began to dissipate. It seemed that her previous resistance to the pain had given it strength, fed it. Now she was releasing that pent up energy and dissipating its hurt. She began to realize that there were alternatives to having the pain. She has sought and used reflexology, jin shin jyutsu and other ancient methods. By allowing the pain, she also allowed new ways of healing into her life.

9. Become a Screen Door to Emotion

Become a screen door to emotions, allowing them to pass through you. When you feel a wave of emotion coming toward you, choose and decide not to clamp down, not to hold your breath. Instead become pliant, a tree in the wind. Open to the experience and imagine yourself, your whole body and being, becoming a screen door. The emotions sweep through you without your attaching to them and getting stuck in them. What you resist persists. Do not resist. Allow. By becoming more transparent and less dense, we allow ourselves to participate in emotions but not to clog up our pipes with them.

As an example, after the movie, I was famished but my friend George had eaten lots of popcorn and wasn't hungry. As we sat down to eat, he was preoccupied and upset, unusual for him. I asked "Do you mind that I'm eating? Are you in a rush?"

"No, take your time," he said but his underlying tension belied his words.

I asked, "Do you have a lot of work to do when you get home?" "Yes." he replied testily.

I was studying *A Course in Miracles* at the time and the lesson that day was, "My present happiness is all I see," about staying focused on the now moment. So I suggested cheerfully "Just forget it. Be here now." It was obvious that was exactly where George didn't want to be and he exploded with, "You always say something like that!"

Totally calm and centered, I wasn't reactive. I felt his anger as pure energy come at me, spiral up and around me, and then pass through me. I was consciously aware of this and continued to remain balanced. I felt the energy as it passed through me but there was nothing for it to attach to. I had become a screen door. It was a conscious decision made in that instant. Astonished, I asked, "Wow, where did that come from?" (referring to George's outburst of anger).

I was processing my reaction to the energy having passed through me. I told George, in a happy, excited way about it. He began to question how it felt and we talked about it. His emotional pattern was interrupted. He shifted out of his angry, judgmental, self-centered state to being amazed and energized. Our experience had just as great an impact on him as it had had on me.

10. *Choose Joy; It's Always a Choice. Just Choose*

Make a conscious decision to have joy. If you find this difficult because you are trapped in a web of emotional pain, remember that joy is not a random event that might "happen" to you but is always available to you, just waiting for you to make it your focus. We hold onto pain because there is some sort of payoff. Until that payoff is met in a healthier way, we will continue to hold on to the pain. This is not a judgment, but just an observation of the situation. If you grabbed a hot poker, you would drop it immediately. There's no payoff. If you do hold onto that hot poker, there is some payoff; perhaps the attention you would receive, ego, superiority, distinction or the need to prove something. These aren't necessarily healthy reasons. There are healthier ways to achieve the same end. For instance, choose something from your Joy List and go do it.

Until something hurts badly enough, we will not change it. It doesn't make intellectual sense because our emotions are running the show. Remember, they are the operating system of the body.

So what is the payoff of holding onto emotional pain? Much of the time, it's martyrdom, attention, sympathy, habit or simply not knowing how else to achieve the same results in more nurturing, loving ways. We don't give ourselves permission to be noticed or to feel our innermost selves. When they can be restrained no longer, our emotional pains overwhelm us and we identify ourselves as actually being them, as in "I AM angry," "I AM grieving," or "I AM betrayed." A healthier way is to acknowledge: "This is anger," "This is grief," or "This is betrayal." Acknowledge it and feel it, but do not identify with, attach to it or become it.

Remember to choose joy. It is always a choice.

In each of the next four chapters we will examine how to apply the principles we have discussed so far to challenges regarding the body, relationships, money and crisis situations. But first, I'd like to share with you a poem by my life partner, Jim Jenkins. He wrote it during a period of intense struggle with emotional pain. He reached within himself and found a way to release his hurt by offering Love, first to himself for being the Creator of the experience, and then to those whom he had previously viewed as causing his pain. It helped him heal. It was his choice.

Choice

I thought of you today, my friend,
as I so often do,
'twas a caring space, a special time,
it brought love into view.

Recalling happy, sun-filled days
like children without fears,
when all was well, carefree and sweet,
and mother dried our tears.

The innocence of childhood past,
we never dreamed would end,
seems lost at times, forever gone,
life's burdens hurt, offend.

But when our heart breaks into halves
from dreadful news or deeds,
we have a choice within our soul
to stop the pain this feeds.

All we ever need to do
at any given time,
is center on the Joys of Life,
our peace becomes sublime.

The focus that we each can choose
determines how we feel.
For what we fear - is drawn toward us,
and what we bless - we heal.

Some might say it's favor, luck,
the label's not the key.
It's Love Without Conditions, yes,
and how we choose to be.

A smile, a hug, a kiss, kind deeds
to strangers that we meet,
will bring much more of same to self
and serve to guide our feet.

Without the hate, or angry words,
nor guilt, revenge or blame,
for judging others holds us back
and only brings more pain.

By loving self, then others, too,
no matter what they say,
releases fears and heartache's pain
while going 'bout our day.

Our cup of joy o'er flows within,
exceeding bliss by far,
when we elect to walk our path
and honor who we are.

(Printed by kind permission of poet and musician Jim Jenkins)

Chapter 8

Our Body Issues

Body Guilt

In our society, the body has become a symbol for lovability, acceptance, approval and self-worth. Advertisements promote the concept that if our body is not perfect according to their airbrushed images, then we are not worthy, lovable or acceptable. We spend a great deal of time rejecting our bodies, demeaning and hating them. If we treated a child the way most of us treat our bodies, with all the horrid focusing on blemishes, fat, birthmarks and baldness, we would not expect that child to ever reach adulthood happy and emotionally unscarred. The negative thoughts and emotions we send to our bodies are no less than emotional and mental abuse. Because of our attitudes, we impose guilt and shame upon the body for its supposed imperfections, its naturalness and its uniqueness.

Here is another way to look at it. We can stop being a victim of the advertising game…or not. It's always a choice. When we loathe ourselves, we play the persecutor and victim portions of the Fear triangle. We may even try to rescue ourselves, or get someone else to do so and tell us we're okay.

Gifts and Bodies

An audience of about 75 awaited the appearance of Philip, a wonderful teacher giving a seminar on our relationship with our bodies. On the stage were many beautiful presents of all shapes, colors, sizes and wrappings. It seemed a festive affair but what did a stage full of presents have to do with our bodies?

All attendees got to *visually* select which of the gifts we wanted, then choose a number from 1-100. We were also told that, of the 100 on the stage, only three had any real value and that no package could be opened till all had been disbursed. Then Philip arbitrarily called those with numbers 60 through 69 to claim their choices first. I was disappointed—the gift I'd wanted, a 6-inch cube wrapped in beautiful reflective gold paper, was taken. The bow was exquisite. I'd always believed that the best things came in small packages and this was a beauty, symmetrical and pleasing to me. I was so disappointed that I kept my eye on that package even though I next selected a larger, identically wrapped package. When we had finished choosing and there were still gifts remaining, Philip recalled a group of ten to choose a second, and so forth until all had been distributed. Some groups had been chosen three times and they then had three gifts. Some had two, most only one.

Philip then asked us to openly reveal our feelings about what had happened so far. As expected, there was excitement, disappointment, jealousy, hurt feelings, in fact, the full range of emotions. The purpose here wasn't to resolve those feelings, just to notice and acknowledge them, to be conscious of how we felt. It may not make intellectual sense, but the body still responds and feels, so we spoke.

Then each group in order of selection was allowed to open their gifts. Of course, I was totally focused on what would have been my first choice. I stood up, straining to see if he'd gotten something I'd have wanted, far more interested in that gift than the one I had in my hands. He opened up my darling, beautiful package and found just a quarter, a simple 25-cent coin. Humph, I thought, and sat down feeling a little smug and glad I still had a chance at a better gift. Finally, my turn came. My package contained a juicer, one of the three valuable gifts. I was elated and humbled at the same time. I felt embarrassed that my friends got such insignificant gifts and mine was so much better. Old self-worth issues surfaced. Simultaneously I wanted to shout how happy I was and hide my embarrassment of riches. At times, our emotions can be so confusing.

The unveiling done, Philip told us that each "gift" represented a quality. The three gifts of monetary value were an espresso machine to a gentleman from Israel who was the most "expressive" student; a deluxe stereo system to the man who did the audio tapings for Philip, and my juicer, reflecting my ability to extract the essence from things.

Most of the gifts were candy, gum, glue or rocks. Oddly, each group of tens had chosen, for the most part, the same contents: that is, the 50-59 group all chose gifts containing glue, the 30-39 group, all gum, etc. It was a subtle but evident example of mass consciousness working in group alignment. The glue represented "love, which is the glue that binds the universe." This is the underlying thread of commonality with all cultures. The candy was for those adding sweetness to the universe. The rocks were for those who were grounding the universe into its solidity, and so forth. None of it was a judgment, just a reflection of individual choice and collective group subconscious.

The analogy was clear. The "gifts" were our bodies. We chose our bodies because of what we thought about at the time we made our selection of our human forms. I'd never really liked my body shape. I felt my hips were too big and my waist too short. I looked like my grandmother, whom I adored and who at 16, was 4' 10" and weighed 165 pounds. Both my sisters inherited my father's long, slim body. They were never overweight in their lives, no matter what they ate. I remember being told, "You'd be so pretty if you just lost a little weight," over and over again, as though this would encourage me. Years later, I realized both my sisters had been underweight as are today's models and that I was actually normal, 125 pounds on my 5' 4" frame. It got locked in my head that I was fat. Slowly I grew into my self-image, adding five pounds every year until I matched my thoughts. It seems therefore that I wanted a pleasing, balanced exterior, but wanted the greatest value within.

We had chosen our gifts based on their shape, appearance, what we believed the contents to be, what was left that hadn't been chosen, or what we perceived others' opinions would be of our selection. A package with wrapping paper that resembled sheets of dollar bills was one of the last to be selected. In the discussion that followed, it became evident that everyone believed that by selecting that package, the audience would think they were money hungry. Could this be why so many of us have money issues in this life? This is exactly why you have your body now. You chose it for specific reasons, to create the rules of your personal "game" in this reality. It serves you perfectly in creating veils to understanding and also abilities to move through those veils in the game of life, and to awaken to remembering who you really are. Claim it. You chose it for a reason with all its challenges and gifts.

Without being judgmental, ask yourself what this was. Listen for the answers and embrace them. Your soul knew what it was doing. Perhaps in your last life you were a stunning specimen of manhood or womanhood.

It caused you endless problems, so emotionally damaging that you vowed that when you got another chance, you wouldn't "handicap" yourself in such a manner again. So this lifetime, you might have chosen another handicap, be it physical, emotional, mental or spiritual.

In choosing our bodies, we got to look them over, decide which we wanted, wait our turn, watch others select the "package" we would possibly have liked, open ours (be birthed), anticipate, be disappointed or pleased.

With this new "ownership" of your body, the conscious self can now determine how to play your hand in this round, knowing it was no accident. Choose joy. Choose love. It's why you came here.

How to Reverse the Process of Body Guilt

Passing a mirror, most of us look only for the flaws, and then focus on them. We do not acknowledge the body's perfection. Its very existence is a miracle and art reflects this. The great artists did not portray only the fit, slim perfect version, but painted and sculpted Rubenesque figures, realistic women such as Mona Lisa, elongated versions such as David, and early Egypt's deformed body of Ahkenaten. Twentieth century art, TV and magazines portray the male and female figures of only one style that represents a minute portion of the population. The human body is beautiful from every aspect.

We tend to focus on only what displeases us, denying the whole while judging and condemning it. We reject it at every turn. It is even difficult for many of us to receive a compliment. We powder, color, de-scent, have cosmetic surgery and hate our bodies. Is it any wonder we have only a 75-year life span? How long can any entity survive emotionally in a healthy manner if it is constantly criticized, judged, demeaned, unloved, rejected, covered up, denied, resented and hated? But this is precisely what we do to our body. It, too, responds.

Remember, we judge in others what we do not yet love about ourselves. Judgment stops the flow of allowing all things to be just as they are and stops the flow of love. Learn to reverse the denial, hatred, and resentment. Give yourself reasons to love your body. Learn to accept that you created it and chose it for the experiences and remembrances it could bring you. Remember those teachings and learn to love yourself. Accept you, and others will, also.

Exercise: Stand naked in front of a mirror. Find 10 things you love about yourself.

Val's Story

Val, a close friend, was going through a divorce. She was in counseling with her husband, who said in a session, "If only you could lose weight, I could love you." She was devastated. She would never be able to please him while his focus was on the physical.

After her divorce, she and I joined a nudist resort, something we had always wanted to do. On our first visit, there were only 3 other people there, all men, and all in the hot tub. She took a liking to one man and they became friends. Afterwards, she said in amazement, "He's already seen me at my worst, wet and naked, and he *still* likes me!"

That realization literally turned her life around by changing her perspective about herself. Of course, we all have preferences, but let's not forget that most of them are learned by socialization.

Obese people are ridiculed and much maligned in the US. But in earlier times, a large body was admired as a sign of wealth and health. Currently in at least one Polynesian nation, a person cannot assume the throne unless their weight exceeds 350 pounds. In Hawaii, it is much the same, where a large body is considered sensual, beautiful.

When you choose fruit in the store, do you pick the skinny one, or the lush, plump, juicy, ripe, sensual one? Of course, we pick the large juicy, delicious ones. In the US, our overwhelming focus on the body has led to one out of 10 women being anorexic or bulimic. To focus on the physical "beauty" is to give value outside of self to a transitory thing. All living physical beauty will fade. So learn to focus on *being* the best you that you can. *You* are the gift to the universe. There can never be another you. You are the only one, unique. Be you. You cannot *do* you, or perform you, just *be* you. Learning who you are, accepting it, loving it, and finally just *being* it is your real purpose here. It's part of our remembering who and what we really are.

Again, we are not talking about selfishness or self-centeredness, but being centered in self. Having flaws is part of the body perfect. Learn to accept them. They are perfect flaws.

On Loving the Body As It Is

If I told you that I used to weigh 435 pounds, had contracted polio as a child, had been burned with a hot pot of water over 40% of my body and had over 17 surgeries to correct a spinal defect, you would be amazed at how well my body functions now. All frailties, infirmities, imperfections and blemishes that once seemed so important would all recede into nothingness in light of the horrors that my body has been through. All these frailties would be overshadowed by amazement and awe at the regenerative properties, the re-formation of wholeness and the exquisite health of this body in its current state.

None of those horror stories about my body is true. Why must we have to undergo drama to be able to appreciate our bodies as they *already are?* Our bodies are our gifts to us. They perform well, are mostly healthy and operate like well-oiled machines. They speak to us if we listen, and tell us what they want. Their senses let us feel, see, think, hear, be, taste, and smell, judgment-free. These are extraordinary gifts. They allow us to feel extrasensory perception, or ESP. The body as is, no matter what its condition, can be honored and loved for itself, perfect, as it was created.

Why then do we focus only upon the flaws, the lack of self-worth? We don't have to have bad things happen to the body in order to appreciate it. Those who have overcome physical challenges look upon their bodies differently and appreciate them wholeheartedly. Do that now. Lovingly approve of your body without having the necessity of overcoming pain or disease. Appreciate your body for what it is, how it can feel, sense, live, connect with divinity, experience itself and the universe. Accept you and you cannot judge others.

Exercise: Choose one cell in the body and love it totally and completely. The rest of the body will get the message of the lovability of the entire body. Just pick one cell. It is so easy to reverse the old pattern. Just one cell.

Death

The fear of death is the ultimate fear of separation. We fear the emotional wrenching of permanent, traumatic detachment from all we love and all who love us. Looking at death from a higher perspective, we can recognize we are being re-birthed into another reality, a greater, more unlimited part of ourselves. Normally we do not consciously choose death. However, we do ultimately create the experience. Remember that we create everything that happens in our lives. Due to the fact that the cause and the effect may be decades apart, it may seem that we did not have a hand in our own death. Long-term illnesses such as cancer, heart disease, arthritis, and diabetes do not happen overnight. Each is the culmination of thousands of thoughts that disrupt the healthy state of the body and cause dis-ease. These destructive thoughts, conscious and unconscious, of self-disgust, self-hatred, shame, guilt, unlovability, and low self-worth are how we destroy ourselves. The cure is to love our self.

Death occurs in each moment of shame, denial and judgment of self and thus is reflected in the body in the form of dis-ease. The true cause of death is not loving ourselves.

Death is a doorway. It is a changing of the form only. The spirit is unchanged. The form is shed. The spirit is free to enliven another form or to remain deliciously unencumbered. Death is a birthing into the next experience. Just as we are in the womb of our mother for nine months, developing our physical form prior to birthing into this reality, we remain in this third-dimensional womb, for an average of 78 years preparing ourselves to be birthed into the next stage. It is simply that. A birthing. Can you imagine a soul being conscious of its newly forming body while in its mother's womb yet believing this womb is its whole reality, that there is nothing beyond its completely cared-for fetal experience?

We do that with this mortal existence. Many believe that this lifespan is the end, that nothing exists outside it or beyond it. Just as the newly forming body in its mother's womb may or may not perceive a state beyond, so, too, we may or may not perceive a state beyond this mortal life. It may be difficult to imagine it since we are so well indoctrinated into fear of the unknown and the limitation that fear brings. Nevertheless, such fear does not preclude the perceptive person's contemplating the possibilities of a further birthing beyond this life.

In death, we will each experience according to the belief system dearest to us. Our creator selves do not cease just because we lay aside the physical form. We are still creating with the etheric emotional body. We do not suddenly have total enlightenment *unless we cross over consciously and are prepared to experience this next aspect of Self.* If our emotional self believes there is a purgatory, a period of being lost, a way stop, stages of passage through the death experience, a need to learn or levels of heaven, we will *tend* to create these experiences. But to the extent that our subconscious and our higher consciousness have prepared us to experience the transition out of physical form and back into our natural, freer, spiritual state, we will then experience the awareness that is the hallmark of this exciting transition. Death is an opportunity to reconnect with our wholly spiritual self and the awareness of our Godself.

When we learn to love ourselves, life and death will be much different. Can you conceive of such fearlessness and such depth of understanding that we can shed or put on any body of our choosing temporarily or for eons, just for the purpose of experiencing the gift of life in such a form? This is exactly what the soul has already done. This is who we already are. The greatest teachers suggest that it is best to remain conscious during the death transition so that we arrive on the other side more aware and having easily shed our limiting forms.

Many times, the death experience seems so terrible. When there is extreme pain associated with such a death and pain-killing drugs are administered to the point of semi-consciousness for an extended period, it becomes an opportunity for the individual to learn how to navigate on the "other side." How else would one who has avoided, denied and ridiculed the thought of an afterlife so easily learn about it and how to exist in it? Painkiller drugs help put the patient in sufficiently altered states to allow for this transition education.

Death is a 'dying of the old form and a birthing into a new experience. We'll all take the ride. We can do so in fear...or not. It is always a choice.

Joy's Death

Joy died. Yes, that really was her name. She had cancer and was heavily drugged for pain. She was my friend and this was a great teaching for me to learn the whys and hows of her illness, her transition and her current state.

In essence, I could say we all commit suicide because there is no real reason to die. We just choose the time and say, "This is enough."

We create the triggering of the "death hormone" and die from it. Death is our incentive to play this game of living. That is to say that if there were no end to the game, where would be the incentive? Isn't a game more fun when there is a final buzzer that goes off, or when there's a time limit? What motivates anyone to action if there is unlimited time? Death is the buzzer in the game of life.

Live for today. Live as though each today is the last day of your life. Grab life. Do. Be. Act. Live. And death becomes a no-thing because life is so exciting. Death is actually the ultimate play in the game of life, the ultimate thrill. If your life is thrilling enough, you do not need to experience death because it holds no excessive fascination. Life does.

In this reality we call our universe, there are Gestalts (a system of rules, accepted perceptions and their behavioral responses). These rules are belief constructs that you must "purchase" to play in our reality. These include believing that time, space and death exist and are real. Believing in them is a prime way to keep this reality just as it is. But things are changing. We are waking up. Growth and awareness are occurring. We are beginning to break down these hard and fast gestalts. For instance, in order to change the gestalt about death, we must get assistance from the dead, from the other side, from those who have had the experience.

This is one of the great benefits people such as John Edward and James Van Praagh provide to mass consciousness. We start the change process from this side by changing our thinking. They are showing us that death is not the end. Because of her changed belief constructs, which she embraced while still alive, Joy is also helping to create a new awareness for the newly dead. She helped anchor the new gestalts about death not being an end to life. This is a new concept of what life is and isn't like after this physical form ends. As more and more dying people join her, having shifted their own consciousness, eventually the belief in death will be broken.

Christ's death provided the same awareness and was done consciously. That was the grand and magnificent difference between how he and most of consciousness at that time approached and entered death. It was a marvelous teaching, but few understood. Even today, most people die asleep to the knowing of where they are going and that they are choosing the experience. They are actually returning to their spirit form, which has awareness (remembrance) of its origin.

FUNERAL: The first part of the word is FUN. Creating a wake or party for the deceased draws their spirit away from its circuitry with the body and lets it more easily detach from it. For a period of about 72 hours, my friend Joy was going in and out of circuitry, the physical electrical connection, with her body. She was having fun with it but didn't yet understand why she could no longer reanimate the body's shell. She did not yet realize she was dead and because she had not yet purchased that belief, she did not put it out into her circuitry. Since others are tied into this same circuitry through love, they cannot yet believe she is dead either. A celebration helps sever that connection with one's body. The message to its spirit says, "Come to the party celebrating the freeing of your spirit from its physical attachment and let's play. Stay away from your body."

If people do not sever the connection, they tend to hang around the body and may experience the embalming process, autopsy or cremation. This is why so many people feel that they were burned at the stake or died in a fire. Many have a recall of their cremation. It may be necessary to connect with their spirit and sever their connection for them. This can be done through prayer or meditation or even dreams.

It is interesting to note here that all the hullabaloo about the "suicide doctor" was about his creating a machine whereby people could consciously choose to sever themselves from this life. This would seem to be a very useful spiritual act. If a person cannot sever that connection and is too attached to the body, a delay may even occur with the funeral arrangements, allowing the spirit more time to disconnect. Allow yourself to "go with the flow" regarding funeral arrangements. Don't fret if they're delayed. The spirit may need more time to disconnect.

The aborigines of Australia consciously choose their time of death, their return to Oneness. This is usually at a very old age. They separate themselves from the group in order to disconnect from the thought circuitry of others that holds them in this reality. Then they begin a quick and systematic shut down of all the body's functions. Within about three hours, they have shifted and died the physical body.

Often a dead person's physical body patterns regarding habits and especially illness may affect others with whom they are closely circuited. This circuitry may allow that undesired pattern to be imprinted on the living person especially during emotionally charged moments such as the funeral. Thus the living person, corded in circuitry with the dead person's pattern, may become ill in the same way—a cough, cancer, diabetes, etc. Through emotional ties, the illness may become imprinted on others. To avoid this, simply stay aware and state your intention that it not be so.

As we progress more and more spiritually, some of us won't even die. We will just disappear from here in the twinkling of an eye but we will be able to pop back in and out. We will leave a hologram here and pop into it. Then the death gestalt will have been truly broken. When 100,000 such people break the old rules (the gestalt), then this will be the Birthing of a truly New Age!

So why stay on? Because of the fun of it. Because of the sheer joy of experiencing one's creations.

Dis-ease

In another aspect of victim consciousness, we declare war on the body every time it goes out of balance. We have the war on obesity, the war on cancer, the war on emphysema, the war on heart disease. When we embrace the concept of murdering an imbalance in the body, we embrace that it: a) is a victim, b) needs to be rescued and c) is wrong. This simply reinforces the out-of-balance condition. The body is never wrong. It is a complete and perfect operating whole. It is simply giving us a physical experience that reflects the emotional experiences and judgmental thoughts we have been bombarding it with for years and in many cases, decades. It takes a good deal of focus on the operating beliefs of our basic thoughts, combined with our emotional energy, to actually manifest something in the physical world, including illness. We say that's magic and only illusion. In truth, the body is whole and remembers its wholeness. It remains perfect in its expression of our underlying thoughts and feelings. Dis-ease is an illusion we have manifested. The mind has created the physical aspect of a dis-ease. The mind can choose to create differently; it can choose to recreate its wholeness once again.

My friend Michael was dying. He had meditated throughout his life and was familiar with altered states of consciousness. The doctors had just told him that his last chance was to undergo chemotherapy. While lying in his hospital bed under the influence of a great deal of morphine, he had a conversation with the out-of-balance cells in his dis-eased body. They appeared to him as small, armed warriors, completely outfitted, like M&M's in suits of armor and battle-ready. They were prepared to resist him-to the death. They wanted to live, too. They were survivors. "But how," he asked them, "can we resolve this matter?"

He offered to negotiate. They consented. They agreed that, if he would not have the chemo that would kill them, then they would agree to exist without doing any further harm to the body. They would be able to peacefully coexist. They would realign with his body and cease their defensive conduct. His job was to accept that all the parts of him were okay, lovable, and created equally, including them.

It was Michael's job to allow and not to judge, to direct his body to accept and make a place for these cells, thus keeping them in balance. He did so and completely regained his health. We need not deny a dis-ease and it is definitely destructive to judge it. Michael realized that, just as with the many dis-eases we already carry within us, it is only when they go out of balance that they become a problem. By choosing to align with a perceived imbalance, we, like Michael, can get the message that is being sent to us and reabsorb that knowledge into our remembered wholeness, the perfection, of the body. All dis-ease is energy. Remove the label of "dis-ease" as "bad" and you have pure energy to redirect. It is your judgment and fear that actually keeps disease alive. You literally give it energy. Choose again. The universe is totally willing to rearrange itself for you. You are the miracle.

If we choose the triangle of Love and put our entire being within it, including what we once deemed separate (the dis eased part), we love ourselves into wholeness.

We see that if we choose out of fear to rescue ourselves by destroying the perceived persecutors in our body, then we create enmity, separation, and a continued physical reflection of the lack of wholeness. Simply dealing with dis-ease in a conscious, love-based way is a path to healing. Creating a war on the body sets it up for resistance, the outcome uncertain. I am reminded of Norman Cousins, who, upon diagnosis of a terminal disease, laughed himself into wellness and wrote about it in "Anatomy of an Illness". He surrounded himself completely with jokes, humor, love and laughter. Doom and gloom were not allowed. He lived because of his decision to love himself and to choose joy.

In our lifetime, each of us really laughs, achieving intense joy with our whole being, an average of only 27 minutes! These are the few times we truly let go and collapse our whole self into joy. Other times, we are observers, standing apart from the experience instead of being inside it, wholly, totally and completely. Think of it: an average lifespan of 78 years and we only spend maybe 27 minutes in total joy. Laughter is our best medicine. Know that you are its source. Add to it consciously. Create joy in your life. It is a choice.

The Immune System

Consider this. The time may come when we no longer need our immune system. When we learn to love ourselves enough, we will no longer create the illnesses that die the body. The immune system will consist of self-love. That love will be prevention enough. We will have learned to captain our own ship (the body perfect) and take care of Self. The Body will reconfigure itself to respond to our love of it instead of resisting our criticism of it. Until that time of course, it remains necessary to use medical resources available to us, both allopathic, the standard Western treatment of disease, and alternative, derived from many different cultures.

Humankind originally didn't need an immune system. Once we were grand and exquisite light beings in our spiritual awareness. As we settled more and more into our bodies, we became denser and denser, moving away from our light-being. We became unloving towards our bodies and in so doing began destroying them with our incessant judgments.

The immune system was created to protect us against our own negative and judgmental attitudes about the body. We can think of the organs of the bodies as planets, universes and other solar systems, with all their individual species. We are the captain and governing body over all these species and universes within. We command the immune system. Instead of responding to physical attack by antibodies and pathogens, we can learn to direct the body's health through our thoughts and feelings. Eventually, we will learn how to control the body this way.

Imagine loving ourselves enough to continually exist in the triangle of Love where we give to Self, receive from Self and accept what we receive to the extent that our love supports the body's remembrance of its perfection. Imagine if we would choose health consistently. This isn't as far-fetched as it may sound. The current method of biofeedback demonstrates the rudiments of using thought and the power of conscious awareness to create one's own health. Imagine thoughts of joy and well-being that immediately create health in the body. What an amazing power we will have but not until we learn how to love ourselves.

If we continue to play the role of victim, we will hate the body into oblivion just as quickly as we would love it into health. We are the creators.

Consider that the time between first thinking a thought and realizing its outcome is shortening so that ultimately we will be creating instantly, but not until we learn to love ourselves, for it would not be safe for us until such time. In order to accommodate this instant manifestation, the whole chemistry of the body may shift. The result will be that, if we are in a state of love, our bodies will instantly create health and remain perfect. If we see hatred, disgust, and embarrassment in the body, we will manifest that also. It is always a choice.

Our Tears

Rajni once said, "Our tears are the diamonds of the universe. In those tearful moments, we touch our very soul and all sentient beings throughout all the universes watch in wonder at ones such as we."

We have unusual responses to tears. I spent many years hiding mine. I rarely cried and usually only in the bathroom with the door closed, but never in front of anyone else, male or female. Tears meant embarrassment. Crying meant vulnerability. They meant weakness. In my mind only weak women cried. I built up emotional walls of control, intellectualizing that *I needed to be strong and tearless* to do business in the world. I believed I couldn't show any trait I considered to be so feminine and weak. I had distorted things so well in my mind that I actually could control my emotions and my expressions. This served me well because I was successful in business. I became manipulative, an observer, distant and I felt superior. I believed that if I acted any other way, I would not be successful. I had built a safe mental construct that served me by denying and then skipping over my feelings. In my mind, people who cried were victims, unable to cope, and weak. I was afraid to cry.

I began to break down this fear little by little. One of Rajni's other students was a wonderful English woman named Eleanor, who cried in almost every class. I used to think *Get a grip. Jeez, lady, what is your problem? Why do you have to cry all the time?* I didn't understand how someone could be so affected all the time, and be so weak. After weeks of this, I finally understood. At one point in the class Raj, addressing me directly, told me something so impacting, so near and dear to me, that my heart overflowed and I was in tears myself, crying in happiness. I finally understood why Eleanor cried. She was so available to her feelings that she was deeply touched in every class. She was able to allow herself to express her feelings and could let tears of emotional release and unlimited joy cascade down her face shamelessly, freely, lovingly. Many years later over lunch, I told Eleanor what a teacher she had been for me. She had always had a self-worth problem and was stunned that she'd been such a great role model for me.

My second step to emotional awakening was to cry in a movie. I had thought that only silly, weepy women cried in movies. Yes, I was often touched by a movie or a good book, but I had the "good sense" to control myself. And that was the problem, *fear of lack of control.* So one day, I allowed myself to cry, wiping tears away before the movie ended. I was taking this in stages. After all, crying had never been safe before. I was really stepping into the unknown with no controls. Then after a few times, I learned it was okay to go ahead and really cry, wiping at my tears on the way to the exit and seeing others who were also crying and connecting with them about how good the movie was. Gee, I realized, they are not belittling me or shunning me, and it's safe because others are crying, too.

The next stage in opening up was to cry in front of my male friends. This was a real challenge because I would really appear weak and out of control and undesirable! However, during a weepy TV show I reached for the tissue...*and so did he!* Oh my God! I was stunned. We were equal. It wasn't a weak woman thing to cry. It really was just an expression of one's naturally sensitive inner self, and he could do it, too. Up to that point, I had only ever seen one man cry, a client who was worried about his daughter. I had never seen my father cry. Not even once!

Oftentimes as we go through spiritual awakening and learn to deal with our emotions in a healthy way, we find ourselves in moments of uncontrolled tears. For many, this will precede feelings of depression or apathy, which is why it's important to focus on what you want in your life. If you feel this way and hang out with unhappy people, your chances of remaining happy are low. If you recognize that you create your own emotions and are the source of them, you can even hang out around depressed people and still not be affected by them. In fact, you may actually have a positive influence on them!

Seratonin: Why Antidepressant Drugs Can Be Useful

Depression can be chemically triggered. In many cases, the body cannot produce sufficient "feel good" chemicals, such as seratonin, to keep feeling good. We have many social prejudices against taking such drugs, and I do not endorse them either long term or on a mass scale. They do serve a valuable purpose, however. I am reminded of a friend who had a severe headache. He meditated, worked with his energy, used all the esoteric self-healing techniques he knew. He called me and asked me what to do. I said, "Take an aspirin."

Self-healing has a place and so does medicine. Here is the story of a young couple in their late 30s who came to me in Calgary, Alberta. She was despondent, subdued and quiet, although she was the one who wanted the intuitive counseling. He was accommodating her, cordial and protective, but with his arms folded over his chest, totally resistant. He said, "I don't believe in all this psychic stuff."

I replied, "That's okay. You don't have to. I do."

The first thing I said to her was, "You are emotionally overloaded, bordering on deep depression."

He sat up stunned and unfolded his arms. He said that he'd just picked her up from 90-days observation stay at a mental hospital. They were clearly worried about her. I told them that she would benefit greatly using an antidepressant drug. Apparently her doctor had just prescribed them for her and this caused them great anxiety. They felt that this was the beginning of the end, that she'd be mentally ill for the rest of her life, always on drugs.

Oftentimes I receive information either through a meditation, through a book or from a friend or teacher that seems interesting, but unusable. It always turns out that this information is for someone else. Just three days before I'd left for Calgary, I'd received such information from a friend about seratonin. I realized that this was the person for whom I'd received that information. After doing my medical disclaimer bit that I'm not a doctor but I will give the information as I receive it, I told her, "You're not broken and do not need to be fixed. This is a temporary condition that should be resolved by using the antidepressant for 6-8 months. The body naturally produces seratonin. It's a brain chemical that helps us to slow down explosive emotional eruptions, and lengthens the time we experience joy. It affects emotions like a time fuse. It stretches them out. Antidepressants retrain the brain to produce a sufficient amount of seratonin to allow us to be more emotionally balanced, less reactive and to stay in joy longer."

She told me, "My doctor didn't take the time to explain these things to us. We thought we were doomed."

In addition to the discussion on how her brain simply needed to be retrained in order to produce more of this chemical and how short a time in which this could be accomplished, we discussed their interaction and fears. We aired their grievances and discussed the 'elephant' that was walking around in their home that both were pretending was not even there. He was scared to upset her so he walked on eggshells. She was afraid of being a burden so she wouldn't ask for anything. They were both stuck in creating a relationship that neither wanted. Once they got permission to be honest, to ask for what they needed, to stop walking on eggshells and to express themselves freely, they changed their lives.

I saw them 6 months later, and every 6 months after that for some time. Allowing themselves to become authentic in their relationship had changed everything. The drugs had done their job, too. She no longer needed them. This couple was electric and excited in their newfound intimacy. Their whole energy had changed. They stopped beating themselves up, stopped fearing each other and their own needs, and lived authentically. They were beaming with joy. I've lost track of them now but often think of them, wishing them continued joy and success.

She had seen herself as both his victim and his persecutor. In her view, he went from being her rescuer when he was nice, to being her persecutor when he became frustrated. From his perspective, she was alternately a victim because she was depressed or his persecutor because she was depressed. They couldn't solve their puzzle. They were lost and drowning in a sea of victimhood. Counseling and a medically administered mood-altering drug became a lifeline, a ladder up out of the snake pit, until they could stand in their own power.

Sometimes we need to take baby steps. It may seem as if we are using rescuers as we climb out of the pit. That's okay. We need what we need until we don't need it any more. Ultimately this couple would realize how they were creating, and begin to choose differently. They used this experience to learn about victimhood and have become powerful, conscious creators.

How Our Bodies Talk to Us

Our thoughts and fears are reflected in our body. So is our love for it. Our wonderful, communicative, physical self is constantly giving us signals as to how our thinking, our fear and our love are affecting it. I severely sprained my ankle one stormy night. An ankle injury is a reflection of one's inability or inflexibility in moving ahead and not taking the next step. I couldn't figure out what it meant at that time. What was I not getting on with? Seven months later, I left my husband. Deep within, my body already knew it. My conscious mind still ignored the signals. Here is another such story.

Bob and Alice were married in late June and had planned a lovely, sunny, outdoor reception. Unfortunately, the weather changed dramatically and it turned cold and windy, so they hurriedly brought the party indoors. They left on their honeymoon and drove to the mountains, stopping to visit her family. Alice fell off a scooter, slamming the palms of her hands into the gravel, stripping the skin. They bandaged her hands but she was in so much pain the newlyweds stayed there that night. After supper, Bob was playing tag with his new in-laws and fell, severely spraining his ankle. They bandaged it, hoping it wasn't broken. They cancelled their honeymoon and went home to heal in their apartment.

The next morning, Bob woke up with extreme swelling in his throat. He had the mumps and was in a great deal of pain. A few days later Alice woke with a severe toothache and had to have an emergency removal of her impacted wisdom teeth. She suggested getting a divorce but their religion prevented it. If ever two people had clear signs that this was not getting off on the right *foot*, that there were things here they didn't want to *handle*, that they couldn't *swallow* what was happening and that there was a *sexual threat* to this relationship, these two people did. Their bodies were telling them, but they weren't listening.

After much pain, Bob and Alice divorced 33 years later. She'd threatened suicide three times. He'd had numerous affairs. She'd sought solace in religion. He was excommunicated. It's no wonder. If they had seen, really seen, what messages they were giving themselves, they might have saved many years of misery.

Bob now says, "It only took a bankruptcy, wrongful imprisonment twice, excommunication, losing two successful businesses, divorce and a five-way bypass before I was ready to change." Alice now says, "He ruined my life."

He woke up and stopped being a victim. She hasn't yet.

We constantly refuse to see our experiences from a higher viewpoint. We ignore the messages because we don't know we can interpret them, much less how to. Perhaps it's time to really see the clues we're getting. The body is continually showing us. But until we're ready, we're not ready.

The Real Fountain of Youth

For centuries we have sought a magical youth potion, convinced it exists somewhere. Many thought it was a real fountain of magical water. Explorers searched for it. Alchemists tried to create it. As with all sources of wisdom, I believe it is found within. It is called Kundalini (pronounced koon-da-lee-nee) and it is real.

Kundalini is an Eastern term for the life force energy that rises through the energy centers of the body called chakras, generally appearing to move up and down the spinal column. Suffice it to say that it is considered the single most potent force in the universe. However, it is not present in full force at all times. Rather, it is often portrayed as a coiled serpent at the base of the spine, waiting to be awakened. Many books are available explaining how Kundalini works and how to awaken and direct it. It is an immensely powerful energy, accessed through either breath, meditation, prayer, yoga, chanting, sex or spiritual focus. It may rise suddenly with little or no preparation. Like many aspects of our world, hot and cold, up and down, in and out, Kundalini also operates in duality, combining both male and female energies. Male energy, called *yang*, is warm and expressed when one is active, doing, achieving, or accomplishing in an external process. Female energy, called *yin*, is cool, such as when one is at rest, allowing, receptive, dormant, waiting, aware and internally processing. For example, eating is yang and digesting is yin.

As it moves up or down in its serpentine manner, one may feel a number of sensations, such as hot and cold. Some have reported unpleasant sensations, usually when there is lack of knowledge, fear, resistance, blockages, or the inability to assist the process when it is out of balance in its pathway. The complete rising of the Kundalini energy leads one to experience *satori*, a blissful state of enlightenment. One's senses are expanded and awareness becomes cosmic. There is an enlivening of each cell as the energy of Kundalini moves through it. As each cell is thus renewed again and again, the body appears to "youthen". Frequent Kundalini activation seems to stop aging. This is a supreme spiritual experience, a reconnection with one's source, divinity, limitlessness, eternality.

As the energy reaches the top of the spinal column, it flows out the top of the head like a fountain, the real fountain of youth. We can direct this powerful electrical energy in positive ways to induce healing, creativity and rejuvenation as we have discussed. But if we misunderstand the energy, we can become its victim. It is important to realize that healing requires the balance of both male and female aspects of Kundalini.

Since ancient times, the symbol associated with the power and movement of this energy is the caduceus (pronounced "kah-doo-say-us"). The medical community long ago adopted this symbol as its own, and it is often seen on ambulances. The straight rod at the center is the spinal column. The two serpentine lines are the male and female energies moving upward. The wings at the top are the spiritual awakening that unfolds.

Many people fear their own personal power because we intuitively know this power is huge. It is the raw life force energy. It is so raw, in fact, that it reminds us of life and of its opposite, death. Think of yourself standing at the base of a huge dam, down near the generators. The tremendous power both thrills and frightens us. The closer we get to power, the more we fear it and are attracted by it. Kundalini is the greatest power source we can touch, the raw energy of the universe, our natural resource available within. We may either choose to be a victim of our power or not. Using our personal and awesome authentic power in joy and love is our natural inheritance in the reflection of God that we actually are.

In order to cease aging, stop blaming the body. Don't accuse it of anything by judging it and being ashamed of it, by wishing it were taller, thinner, blonder, bigger here or there, lighter or darker. Love it just as it is. We train our bodies to feel unloved and limited. We begin the death process by repeating these self-destructive comments over and over. ***Argue for our inadequacies and we get to keep them.***

Each night as you go to sleep, evaluate your day. Ask yourself, "Did I have joy today? Did I live today?"

Have no wasted moments. Grab life! Then death is no thrill. It holds no excitement because you seized each moment. Grasp aliveness on a regular basis. Each morning when you awaken ask, "Will I have joy today? Will I really live today?" Now choose.

Exercise: When you wake up in the morning laugh for two minutes. Note your approach, resistance, involvement and enjoyment..

Body Secretions and Excretions

Our culture teaches that every thing issuing from the body is disgusting. From earwax and phlegm, to sweat and feces, our natural emissions are judged as revolting, smelly, untouchable, unmentionable. These are products that every normal body discards in order to cleanse itself or to release itself, yet we allow them to be an embarrassment. Our bodies receive this message and respond to our constant judgment. Our opinions are learned. We teach the body that it is not acceptable or lovable. No wonder we have such a hard time learning to love ourselves. We have made our bodies victims of their humanness and their perceived imperfections. We can change this process, however. We can learn to love ourselves once again.

Loving Your Femaleness

For years I hated my monthly menses. Ever since I was a child, I'd had extremely difficult menstrual periods that were lengthy with painful cramps. They were irregular in arrival so it was often a surprise. Oh joy. What is there to like about this, I wondered. As I was to learn, a great deal. If I continued to hate the most female part of myself, then I was hating the part of me that was nurturing, creative, able to receive and allowing. I was a victim of my own femaleness.

During a lovely meditation one evening, a diminutive Chinese lady appeared to me. She was regal, calm, centered, elegant and soft-spoken. She talked to me of my feminine energy and my femaleness. She spoke of the moon, saying, "It is beautiful because it reflects the sunlight, which is solar, male energy. Its receptivity is its only 'action' and by such passiveness does it attain its highest purpose. The moon has no light source of its own. It has a cycle, dependent upon the male energy of the sun. The moon is a dark hunk of rock. It can only be receptive and reflective of the sun's light, yet it causes the oceans' tides to be drawn to it due to its innate nature of attraction and gravity. Simply by being, the Moon is responsible not only for the tides, but also for the calendar months, crop planting schedules, menstrual cycles, fertility, time itself and birth. Thus the moon is a perfect example of the interaction of male and female energies that unite to create life. By doing nothing, it accomplishes everything."

The Chinese lady also said, "You need to honor your feminine side more and honor your womanhood, including your moon-time (menstrual period). Instead of feeling, 'Oh no, not again,' rejoice in the reactivating of the nurturing female energy within." This also applies to men's attitudes about women's menstruation. Men often feel as though they are its victims, too.

From that moment, I never again felt like a monthly victim of my body and I understood female energy in a whole new way.

Summary

We chose these bodies. We can choose to go along with the crowd—the advertisers, the doctors and our old teachers—or we can be the creators of physical change in our magnificent self. We can youthen or age gracefully…or not. It's our choice. Our fears are what limit us and they determine to what extent we participate in our own health and our body's physical experience. The alchemists of old sought to make gold out of lead, but they were really attempting to change the physical body into its highest spiritual self. Such a journey is assisted by learning to love ourselves, all of the Self, including that which appears imperfect.

We can either be a victim of the experiences of the body, an observer, a persecutor, a judge, or we can create experiences out of love. We can choose to love ourselves or not. The choice is ours; so are the results.

Chapter 9

Dealing With Relationships

Why We Choose Friends and Mates

We each wander around with a partially filled cup of love, bringing people into our lives in hopes they can fill it for us. Subconsciously, we perceive the source of love as outside ourselves and seek others to make us feel loved. This is how we give others the power-our power – to "make us happy" and set ourselves up for victimhood.

The *real* purpose of any relationship, but especially a mated relationship, is to create the highest aspect of who you can be in a loving, non-judgmental experience. It is a journey for the self. Self can be more easily discovered when it is relative to something else, just as we can best understand the concept of high by comparing it to low. A union is not for learning what makes the other person happy and then changing our lives to fulfill him or her. Remember, we can't make anyone feel anything. We are not responsible for anyone else's feelings, but we may be a trigger for them and they for us. We get to look at what pushes our buttons while existing in this loving space that both have created. We draw to us a person with the particular triggers that will assist our own growth. A relationship is about the Self, not the other, not the two of us, not the relationship itself.

We are whole, complete and perfect before we ever enter a relationship. We do not need a relationship to make our life complete or to find our "other half." We have our own complete power and ability to love ourselves.

You Are The Source of Love

A relationship is a multidimensional connection. In other words, you are in this union for more reasons than your limited human self thinks. You are in it to experience more of your unlimited spiritual Self. If you are focused outside yourself in a relationship, then it is because you fear that you are not lovable and you seek validation and love from others. Your journey then is to *real*-ize, to make real, that you are the source of love. It is within you. Your soul's desire is to be love, to make it real.

We are in a relationship to discover who and what we want to be. Relationships are about *ourselves*, not about the other person. We get to be ourselves. The other person gets to be him or herself. We can each discover new things about ourselves. Think back to a time when you first began a relationship, either a friendship or a romance, and took a risk by revealing something about yourself. When you continued to reveal, take risks and get approval, it was exciting. You felt accepted, loved. Then one day, or one moment, you realize that you may have invested so much in this connection that you can risk no more. Your mate has accepted you up to a point but may not love you if you revealed all of who you are.

The problem is often that we don't love our whole self enough to really be present in the relationship. We can't be authentic. Deep within, we feel unlovable, unacceptable. So we begin to deny ourselves, to hide parts of us, to validate that the entire package of self is not lovable. After all, we justify to ourselves, who would possibly love us if they knew everything about us?

The end of risk-taking in a relationship is the beginning of its death. From then on, it's just treading water, hiding who we really are, denying our preferences, cutting off pieces of ourselves, pretending that we can do without them. It's just that an end isn't visible yet. For instance, suppose your mate dislikes Chinese food, which is your favorite, and refuses to ever go to a Chinese restaurant. So you say to yourself, "That's okay, I can live without Chinese food."

Or perhaps your mate doesn't like it when you wear shorts, so you find yourself giving that up, seeking approval, withdrawing from the judgment when you wear them. Little-by-little, you give up parts of yourself while the Self is crying out, "When is it my turn?" or "Notice me, please."

Often couples begin case building against each other to create enough ammunition to have a real reason to eventually disconnect and get a divorce. If you were to become the authentic you and really be you, the outcome of the union would be different. The games would cease. The manipulation would end. Feelings long repressed would be aired. This doesn't mean that everything would be magically perfect. It does mean however that the playing field would be leveled and communication would be real. Choices would be easier to recognize and change could be embraced. Guilt and blame would cease because both parties would know they are each responsible for their own emotional journey.

The moment the parties shift their main focus to the other person and their feelings instead of their own, they have begun to destroy the relationship. Awareness and compassion for another's feelings are totally appropriate but making them the sum focus of your life is unhealthy. It can be so much easier to deal with someone else's feelings if you don't have to deal with yours. In focusing on the other person, you make him or her someone whom you must be careful of, take care of, or fix. That makes him or her a victim. It says, "You aren't really capable of taking care of your own life and feelings, so I'll do it for you." It sets you up as the rescuer and you begin crippling your beloved. Find healthy ways to work with emotions when they come up but don't live your life in anticipation of or preparation for them. Such healthy releases may include getting counseling, setting a timer while you take 20 minutes to vent or cry, or beating a rock with a rubber hose. There are many positive ways to release.

Remember, we create all of our own feelings, not some of them or some of the time, but all of them all of the time. We come to this world with our hidden enemies (teachers). By this I mean that we create the people in our lives who push our buttons so that we can move past our fears. Then we blame them when, instead, we should thank them for performing on our stage and in our play with us and reminding us what we came into this life to surmount, or that limitation we needed help with to get past. They are that help. They can keep us on track and help us to progress on our spiritual path … or not. It's always our choice.

A person may seem obnoxious to you but, from a higher perspective, you can see that same person as a benefactor. For instance, the smoker that lights up right next to you in a restaurant may at first seem to be your persecutor. If you acknowledge that you create all your experiences and are willing to listen to that still small voice within then, when something like this happens, you already know it has a reason for happening. Listen for that internal guidance to reveal the reason. Recognize that the event is in your highest interest. Sometimes you may not know what that reason is; sometimes it becomes blatantly

obvious. You ask yourself, "What do I want to do about this smoker?"
You want to change tables but you feel too self-conscious. Soon, a
waiter serving the adjoining table trips and spills tomato sauce all over
you. Your anger, ultimately at yourself for not taking the opportunity
to make things better for you was like a magnet drawing more and
more frustration and victimhood triggers.

If you had chosen to give to yourself and change tables, the incident
might have been totally avoided because you were staying in the flow,
creating from your joy and not as a victim. In fact, by actively choosing
joy for yourself a whole different scenario may unfold. For instance,
you notice you left your wallet at home but you are gifted with a free
dinner because you were the thousandth patron since the restaurant
opened, or some other equally unexpected honor. Try it some time.
Stay out of judgment and victim-hood when a mini-disaster occurs.
Don't personalize it. Allow it all to unfold, without expectation. Look
for the silver lining. You will begin to create your own miracles.

Soulmates

If you believe a mate will appear who is the answer to all your dreams,
who will be your other half and make you whole, who will love you
the way you desire, and who means everything to you, chances are you
are in for great disappointment. You have put a great burden of
responsibility on his or her shoulders and made him or her responsible
for your happiness and your disappointment. You have taken on the
role of victim and you await your rescuer. If you define a soulmate as
one who appears in your life to remind you of the existence of even
just one facet of who you really are, then you have a sense of the true
meaning of the word. Thus one can have many soulmates; male, female,
child, adult. Being a soulmate is not a condition of intimacy, but rather
a spiritual connection that reminds you of your wholeness and Oneness
with all that is.

In my work, I see many victims of this thinking who await that one perfect "soulmate." We become victims of ourselves. We actively play all three parts (victim, persecutor and rescuer) all by ourselves. .

We have bought into the belief system that says, "A knight in shining armor or a virgin princess will find me and I will live happily ever after in some fairy tale way. Okay, maybe I'll have to make some minor adjustments but, since it's a soulmate, it'll all turn out perfectly and we'll live happily ever after. After all, we'll just have to be together. We were meant to be together."

Hogwash! This belief is based on two premises, both flawed. One is that we need rescuing in order to be "complete." That tells the world and ourselves that we are incomplete and must find our "other half" in order to be happy. The second is that we're placing joy outside ourselves and making someone else responsible for supplying it.

Often we just sit, lonely, heartbroken and fearful that we're unlovable except by this fantasy love whom we must await in hopes he/she finds us. We go to intuitive counselors hoping they will reveal the name, circumstances, address and phone number of this supposed Mr. or Ms. Right. We thus give away the responsibility (and our power) for creating such a being in our reality to neighbors, coworkers, roommates, clergy, matchmakers, singles groups, parents, friends and psychics. We create relationships with that special someone based on who we already are. Love isn't about *finding* the right person; it's about *being* the right person.

If you are Mr. or Ms. Waiting in Dreamland, then you are holding off meeting a potential mate or oblivious to anyone who doesn't exactly match the qualities of your dream mate. Develop those qualities in yourself that you desire in your dream mate. Become them and you will then magnetize such a person to you.

The Mirror Of Our Fears

We draw to ourselves a reflection in a mate that best shows us our fears so that we may move through them and become the highest spiritual self we can be. In taking responsibility for creating our reality we begin by creating in ourselves the qualities we desire in a mate, business partner or friend. We magnetically attract to ourselves those who will reflect our true nature to us. This is why an abused woman draws an abuser to her. She feels such an extraordinary lack of self-worth that she can only create another being in her world who has that same inability to see her value. It is a perfect mirror in this regard. It reflects her fears. But she can change it.

The Fantasy Mate

So many people sit around hoping that someone will rescue them and love them. They cut themselves off from life and love, thinking they are unworthy or unlovable. They have unrealistic perceptions of what relationships look like, mostly developed from romance novels, TV and movies. They see little white picket fences around a darling cottage, or a luxurious mansion, and a mate who takes care of all their needs, physical, mental and emotional, without ever having to ask. They're just supposed to *know*. Rubbish!

You are not a victim waiting around to be rescued. You are the creator of your waiting around! Your self-worth and lovability are not determined by anything outside of yourself. As long as you look for these things outside of you, you will create relationships that just don't stand up in the long haul. They can't because they were based on a dream whose illusion cannot be maintained in the long term.

Eventually, those rosy glasses need washing and the true nature of idealized mates comes to light. They fall off the pedestal you placed them on. Their all too human frailties and fears can no longer be suppressed and they become needy, hostile, overbearing, controlling, judgmental, demanding, withdrawn or depressed. They are reacting to being the rescuer in someone's life. They themselves wanted rescuing and they are not getting the attention they desperately need. They, too, placed the responsibility of feeling good, safe, wanted, loved and happy in another's hands, outside of themselves. The only problem is that both chose victims who were unwilling to give to themselves. Thus, both give away their power, always secretly hoping that if they perform well enough, it will be their turn to receive. The one they started out rescuing becomes their persecutor. Over and over, we get trapped in playing one of the roles, then another, then another. But we can shift out of this cycle.

Create-A-Mate List

To create the relationship you want, first make a list of the emotional qualities you desire in a mate. Forget the physical attributes or any other qualities having to do with form. Then *be* the emotional qualities on your list. Make sure that if, for example, your list has the qualities of being emotionally available, communicative, happy, balanced and generous, that you are emotionally available, communicative, happy, balanced and generous. If you are not these things, then your energy is sending out messages that block attracting them in a mate. Become the person you'd like to have in a relationship with you, and your energy will exude attraction to such a mate. This works just like a magnet, attracting who you are. One of the best ways to look at our own issues is to ask, "Whom have we drawn into our lives?" Take a look at these people and see how they reflect aspects of you. Decide if you wish to continue drawing such friends. Make changes in yourself if you do not.

Create A Mate

There are many ways to create a perfect mate in your life. First, remember that this perfect mate may be only for a short term. "Perfect" does not have to include "for ever." If, as you read the words "short term," your heart and breath stop, then look at your issues around permanence and your need for it. Stay open, allowing and flexible. Secondly, begin to recognize where your fears are in having a relationship. For example, many clients ultimately confess that they believe they'll lose their freedom, or become servant, laundress, cook, caretaker or open checkbook for a spouse. Those who have lost a loved one may fear the emotional trauma of losing another, so they keep relationships away and remain alone. Look at your own fears first. These are the vibrations you are sending out to others. When you realize what you're projecting, you can easily see why you don't have a mate or why you have one you don't want!

We must first become the person we want to *be with* in a relationship. If you want an open, expressive mate, then become open and expressive yourself. Look at how you are stating your hopes, wishes and dreams in your create-a-mate list. "I don't want ." statements in your list reveal that you're really focusing on what you don't want. These are your fears talking.

Remember to state your preferences with a list of emotional qualities, not physical ones. Your list might look like this:

"I choose to have a mate who is:

> emotionally available,
>
> generous,
>
> allowing,
>
> nurturing,
>
> has resolved money issues,
>
> able to communicate,
>
> independent and
>
> who loves him or herself as much as he or she loves me."

If you seek only a "tall, dark, handsome man" or a "slim, blonde, beautiful woman," you may miss out. You are limiting yourself to a specific form. Stay away from form on your list. If your mate had all the emotional qualities listed above, would you really put that much value in how he or she looked?

Exercise: Make a list of emotional qualities you desire in a mate. Then ask yourself if you yourself are those qualities. If not, become them. This will be a process, not just an intellectual decision. Remember, we are talking about emotions here, not just the head, but the heart and soul.

No matter what it is that you want to have in your life, it is possible to obtain it by magnetically drawing it to you. Once you become the person you want to have in a relationship, your energy becomes magnetic to that type of person. Just by sitting in your living room, loving yourself, being responsible for creating your own life and the people and things in it, you can have all your desires. Here is one such story.

A Modern Fairy Tale

Once upon a time, not so very long ago, high on Grouse Mountain overlooking Vancouver, Canada, a lady rebuilt her life and was most content and satisfied with what she had wrought. Although lonely at times, she would let no man get close and her new life was happy, secure and full. Her name was Holly.

At the same time, a gentleman saw his life dissolving around him and he retreated from his native land to the ancient village of Aniane, deep in the south of France. Here he began to create a new life, one where he would live alone and need no one. His name was Jeremy.

And so it came to pass that very, very late one evening, Jeremy became lonely and called to chat with his favorite cousin who lived in Canada. An unknown woman's voice answered and Jeremy said, "Sorry, I think I dialed the wrong number."

She replied, "Yes, I think you did," and prepared to hang up.

"Do you want to talk?" he asked.

She wondered, *what kind of a weirdo do I have here?*

He repeated, "Do you want to talk?"

Being a polite lady, she responded in the affirmative and somehow they ended up in a conversation. More than four hours later, when the sun had come up in Aniane and the sun had gone down in Vancouver, two very mystified people realized their beliefs had been shaken. Something very rare and unusual had occurred.

The next day, both wondered if it had been real or a dream. So Jeremy called again. Once again Holly answered. This time they spoke for seven hours, and it was very, very good. They continued to speak daily and the relationship deepened. On Valentine's Day, he sent her an extravagant bouquet and she was both afraid and angry at the joy that welled up in her heart. Still they continued to talk and laugh as each secretly came to feel more for the other than was spoken aloud, or even admitted privately in the depths of their souls.

One day, Holly was reading a note from Jeremy and heard her voice say, "I surrender," and she knew she loved again and was terrified. Quickly she denied it and hid the feelings. She would not and could not admit it. During another phone call, an endearment slipped unbidden from her lips and he pounced on it. "What did you say?" he asked.

Twin dams broke as mutual love was brought into the light. A few days later, they planned a meeting in Vancouver. They agreed that he could stay in her guest room. After all, if it wasn't real, he could write it off as a business trip and little would be lost. You can see that these were two very practical people. No expectations were allowed, at least on the surface. Fear simmered, for both knew that this situation was impossible, illogical, impractical and ridiculous. Yet neither could bury nor deny the hope and happiness that blossomed within their hearts. Doubt ran high. What would they say to each other? How would it all work out?

They met at the airport. They walked arm-in-arm to a neutral place to get acquainted with seeing each other in physical form. They laughed in pleasure, joy and relief. The visit was beyond their wildest dreams. She soon traveled to France to see if she could live there. The land spoke to her heart. It felt like home. They decided to look for a home to live in, and one appeared the next day without searching or striving. Shortly after that, they were married in Canada and now live in joy in the South of France.

This is a true story. Holly and Jeremy have just purchased a home in a charming village just north of the Cote d'Azur. They are celebrating their third anniversary and living their fairy tale.

Life is about *being*, not *doing*. By being open, they both created a space between, where possibilities exist and can become reality. We all get to choose.

Intimacy Without Sex

So often we think that, unless an intimate partner wants us sexually, we are unlovable or undesirable. In losing our healthy perspective and embracing our victim selves, we lose the option of seeing the relationship for what it does offer. Intimacy can be just as satisfying as sex. It's just different.

A gentle friend once said to me, "Think out loud," as we were waiting for another friend. It was a lovely comment, saying he wanted to share intimacy with me. He wanted closeness by my communicating my inner thoughts. I shared with him exactly what I was reflecting on. How often when someone says, "What are you thinking?" do we quickly say, "Oh, nothing," as though we've been intruded upon. We fear being authentic. We fear vulnerability and we miss opportunities to see and love ourselves. How small a thing it is to share yourself with another and how wondrous. How big an issue it can become when you don't.

In another setting, Catherine wanted physical contact with the man she loved. She wanted to make love but he was impotent. There were obstacles and she was frustrated. Believing in staying in the flow of things, she allowed it all to unfold without demands, shoulds or have tos. Her lover had been quite ill, actually having a near death experience and had considerable muscle toxicity. She offered a massage. All that pent up desire for sexuality was redirected into touching his body and transmuting and releasing tension with total focus. Catherine felt greater and greater depth of connection. She achieved a semi-trance state akin to meditation when she opened up and redirected her own Kundalini energy channels into the work on him. This was a thrilling awareness, one Catherine would have missed if she'd unhappily accepted the absence of the usual sexual event.

Family

Families can be both the most painful and most joyful of all long term relationships. In them we often have as much deep hatred as we do deep bonding. Try this perspective on for size. What if we actually chose our family when we were still in spirit form and made our choice from the highest level of our being? If we believed this we could perhaps stop being victims of our family dynamics.

We'd see that we chose these very family members to have all our buttons pushed, get unstuck and become the best "us" possible. We were creators, not victims in this undertaking. Who can get under our skin more than family members? By remembering that we asked for these grand teachers in our lives and that they are here to move us past our biggest blocks, we can get on with our greatest growth and not get stuck in recrimination. We may eventually thank them for pushing us, kicking and screaming, into freedom, growth, self-awareness, self-love, self-empowerment and into our highest possible selves.

Here is the story of a loving, committed family man who divorced after 33 years of marriage. As he began to wake up, he learned that the love in his family had been very conditional. After the divorce his "loving" family turned their backs on him. His ex-wife donned the role of victim and he was cast as the persecutor. Healing wasn't allowed. Victim she chose and victim she will remain, until she chooses differently. It is an option.

Theirs had been an unusually close, intimate, religiously based family. Children meant everything. When both his married daughters became pregnant, he was left out. Upon delivery, one daughter called and he shared her delight and joy, but his involvement ended there. Even today, he is not allowed to see any of his grandchildren. Accidentally, he learned that his other daughter had given birth only five miles away and still he was excluded. This caused him untold anguish and grief. However, instead of hating, judging and remaining in pain, he decided to transmute it by directing and focusing all the energy of his feelings into love. He sat down and wrote this poem. A musician, he later set it to music. He sent that poem to the beloved daughter and it, too, went unacknowledged. Here is that pain, clearly transmuted. There is no victim here.

Daughter

There are priceless moments, my dear child,
While we are here on earth,
But none can equal, nor surpass
Your own new daughter's birth.

It doesn't seem that long ago
I held you in my arms,
In awe-struck wonder, joy and bliss.
I feel it still; it warms.

With "Clouds of Glory" did you come,
From unseen time and place
Where angels dwell, so we believe;
I saw it in your face.

Your tiny hand grasped fingers firm
As you reached out to nurse.
How did you know so much, so soon?
Did someone teach? Rehearse?

Oh yes, my child, your daughter knows
Exactly how to be.
She's full of love, and has no fear.
Not yet like you and me.

And as you gaze into her eyes
While fighting back the tears,
Know this: The best is yet to come
As days turn into years.

Love, Dad, May 27th, 2001

Unfinished Business with My Dad

Unlike the father who wrote the above poem, my dad was not a feeling man. In fact, I'd only seen him kiss my mother twice, both times on demand and both times he'd made a joke out of it. No wonder I'd grown up with shut down feelings. I'd never been close to him and around age 11, something happened. From then on, I plain just didn't like him. I didn't know consciously exactly what happened, but my dislike became intense.

Jumping ahead to age 40 and many years after his death, I was seeking understanding and healing of this relationship. I journeyed in a meditation and got my answers. Now, you may say that it was just a head-trip, a phony made-up story. You may be right. But whatever helps us to understand a thing or see it from a new perspective or resolve emotional turmoil is helpful. In other words, whatever works, works.

My meditation showed me that in a past life, he was a Mayan priest and, at age 11, I had been his sacrificial victim. It finally all made sense. Somehow, somewhere, there was a dormant and intense recall. Forcibly taken, I was placed face up on the sacrificial altar. His two hands grasped the ceremonial knife high over his head. Our eyes locked. In that instant, he experienced conscious awareness and remorse over what he was doing. As he plunged the dagger into my chest, wordlessly, yet emotionally, he communicated to me that he knew he would have to redeem himself with me in a later life. This was that life.

He was staying in a loveless marriage, providing for his children and wife. He had urged my mother to have an abortion when she carried me. They had fought. Somehow he knew that this was the difficult relationship about to be birthed and he wanted out at the last minute. But he'd married a Roman Catholic and there would be no abortion.

So the relationship went sour at age 11. I despised him. Now, at age 40, I learned how to forgive and to love, and healing began. I'd stopped being his victim. What terror and horror he must have known when he realized that he, a gentle person, would have to face the child he murdered and resolve the unspoken conflict. Well, it never did happen while he lived but we had created a way for it to come about.

We are not victims of karma, supposed unpaid emotional obligations from previous lives. This story is meant to illustrate how we can become trapped in thinking we are, unless we choose not to be.

More importantly, it is meant to illustrate that we can go back into the past, get our answers and re-script our lives. We are unlimited beings. If, by re-writing our past lives or even our current lives, we can release our fears and bring forth love, then by all means use past lives to do so. The funny thing was that my father actually believed in past lives. I only learned after his death that he'd once told my mother that he distinctly recalled being trampled to death by an elephant in a former life.

Whatever works, works.

Who Is the Persecutor?

You hate your alcoholic father. You threw the abuser out at age 18 and took over providing and protecting your family. Now this certainly qualifies as victim-persecutor-rescuer! But who is who?

Mom and you are the victims. Dad is the persecutor. You are the rescuer. However, Dad was a victim of his parents, siblings, employer, family's needs (fill in the blank). If Dad was a victim, then he saw his wife as his rescuer (she was supposed to love him), and the kids as his persecutors (they had constant demanding needs that he had to fill). His boss at work was probably a victim (if you see it from the perspective of having an alcoholic employee). But Dad may see his boss as the persecutor driving him to drink. If you are thoroughly confused by now, that's just the point. It's not easy separating the roles once we begin to play the victim game.

The point here is that we play all the parts, each of us, until we decide to stop. Either everyone is a victim or no one is. Either everyone around you is a persecutor or everyone is a creator. If you take the perspective that no one is a victim, then you can begin to get a glimmer of your own personal power. You can begin to see that you are the creator. You can begin to see where your own fears are and how you create scenarios that offer you an opportunity to move past those fears by seeing them, getting immersed in them and waking up to their real purpose and value.

Twenty years after this scenario, Dad stopped drinking, remarried and changed considerably. But, oh no, you don't want to hear that! You want to hold him in his cage, the one you created in your mind's eye. He is an abuser. He is an alcoholic. He is a persecutor. But this holds you, too, in your own cage called "victim," an adult child of an alcoholic and afraid of being genetically predisposed to the same conduct. In addition, you may consider yourself a victim of what you internalized from learning by example in regards to how you treat a mate, your children, and all others around you. So you don't forgive him; you don't acknowledge that he has changed; you don't let him back in your life. You hold on to those fears, that hatred ... until it no longer serves you. It has fueled you and been of service to you in some way or it would no longer be a part of your life.

So how *does* it serve you? Take all the judgment labels off your thinking and let's look at what may be going on.

First of all, you were probably intimidated by your dad. By debasing him or pigeonholing him, you can at last feel superior. You can't let go of that hatred because then you won't feel superior. (Fear of lack of self-worth.)

Second, you fear that you could be just like him because you have a tendency to tip the bottle, too, and have seen yourself drunk. Your hatred of him covers up that terrifying fear that you might just be like him. You think that, if you hate him enough, you'll prevent yourself from being like him. You hang on to that hate. (Fear of lack of control.)

Third, if you refuse to acknowledge that he has changed, you can punish him and make him a victim... at long last. So you play persecutor, while tricking yourself into believing that you are protecting yourself and your family from "HIM" and his old tricks. Hang on to that belief that he can't be trusted. Punish him some more. Don't let go. (Victimhood consciousness. I'll make you the victim, I'll play the persecutor, all Fear Triad.) This is reminiscent of adolescent behavior such as, "He hit me so I'll hit him back."

Learn to Allow

How do you break out and let go of being a victim? How can you accept Dad in his new life? Simple. Allow, allow, allow. Allow yourself to see differently and allow him to be different. You don't have to give up any part of the old feelings or memories—they're real. The feelings were real. Expand your awareness to include seeing more of who he is and more of who you are. Just choose to focus on new feelings. Don't unearth old wounds to rebirth yourself. Shift your focus. Get on with a new day. Focus on what you'd like in your life. You'd like a dad you could respect, one you could love, feel safe with, trust. So, respect what you can. Love what you can. Feel safe within yourself. Love yourself. Trust yourself. Then you can display those feelings to him, but first they must grow and thrive within you.

When you Love yourself: you Give to yourself, you Receive from yourself and you Accept what you have given to you. When you view life from a higher perspective, realizing that you and others are one and you can love *yourself*, you can then also love your dad. When you feel safe in your own being, you can feel safe with others. It is all an outward projection of who you are inside.

Mothers

My mother is now 90 years old and in a care home. Our relationship has not always been good. In fact, at one point, I even evicted her from one of my rental homes. Relations were strained at that point, to say the least. I initiated contact with her again after a 10-year hiatus. I'd changed dramatically. I was a different person with a totally different perspective. It takes such a cataclysmic break and a remarkable new bonding to change the dynamics in parent-child relationships. If she didn't want a relationship, that was okay, too, but it did begin again and everything was different. I became my mom's teacher. The old paradigm was broken. The old angers were shifted. Everything is a choice.

Seeing God

One day after renewing the relationship with my mother, I was talking on the phone with her. She was upset and vilifying one of my sisters. I had about all I could take and asked myself, *what's going on here?* As she continued, I took it step-by-step and asked myself, *how do I feel about this? Abused, put upon, overloaded, angry and full of resentment,* I answered myself.

What do I want to do about this?

Put a stop to it, I advised myself.

But how? I asked.

"See her actions as fear-based," I told myself. "This is clearly fear of lack of control and fear of being unloved. I can acknowledge those fears and see them in the intensity of her conversation. I can choose to see her as an aspect of God, who has simply forgotten who she really is, being afraid and needing love. In this moment, I choose to see her as God."

And then something extraordinary happened. I *felt* a warmth and light come over me. I felt her Godhood as a flood of light from within. I loved her and merged with that love. I felt as if I'd seen God, and it was because of her. In that same instant, she stopped in mid-sentence. Everything suddenly changed. She said, "Well, I guess that's enough of that! I'm going to stop talking about your sister and change the subject to something pleasant."

Without my *doing* anything, the perfect result occurred. I'd had no agenda; I was simply in the feeling of seeing God. The simultaneity amazed me. I later realized that if I had continued to be angry at her conduct, I would have added fuel to the fire and her pattern would have continued.

What does this story tell us? That our emotions and thoughts count. That they have real effects, although we often choose not to be responsible for them. Because the results of those mostly unconscious, creative thoughts and actions are often very distant from the cause, we can easily fool ourselves into believing we are not creators. But by choosing consciously how to perceive, and by *consciously* choosing love, huge changes can be instantaneous.

Guilt

We learn guilt at our mother's knee. Putting guilt trips on them are easy ways to control, coerce and modify the behavior of children from a very early age. It begins as soon as a child can sense and interpret the emotions of others. "Don't do that. You wouldn't want Mommy to feel bad, would you?" Or, "Stop that. When you behave like that, I'm ashamed of you."

We are thus taught to *feel* responsible for how others *feel* and that we'll *feel* horrible if they don't live up to our expectations. In other words, we and they must act in ways that will make others *feel* good and not *feel* bad. These are atrocious teaching techniques, efficient yes, but dreadful in their long term consequences. They are among the first emotional imprints on our subconscious. They teach that we are responsible for making others feel good and that if we don't meet others' expectations, we are unlovable. This is the great fear-based web of lies that entraps us, which we subsequently spend a lifetime undoing. The infant being trained into these anxieties is doomed to an existence of pleasing others first, driven by externalized self-worth and fear of unlovability.

More negative reinforcement comes along as children learn, time and time again, that life is about how we take care of others and, in the process, put self last. This message is usually conveyed by the parent's example. At age two, we have already become a persecutor and our poor dear mother is the victim. It may shift in the blink of an eye as our behavior changes. We may be the victim and she, or Daddy when he gets home, becomes the persecutor. "You just wait until your father gets home," is the sword of Damocles held over many a child's head, who gets to wait, terror-stricken, for a good long while before the persecutor's arrival.

We get really entrenched in creating fearful feelings that imprint the subconscious. Undoubtedly the child will be in these fear-based feelings for more than those 17 seconds it takes to shift our electro-magnetic field (as discussed in the Chapter 7, Ten Ways to Choose Joy). It is indeed a difficult trap to escape, both for the parents and the child.

Instead of using guilt, try reinforcing a child's behavior (or anyone's for that matter) as they accomplish something well. Hearty approval and lavish praise for behavior also go a long way to boosting self-worth. This also works with adults. If adults were consistently validated with honest, non-agenda praise, that is, praise for a job well done, regardless whether the results accrue benefit to you or not, there would be fewer wounded people causing havoc in order to get a sense of self-worth.

Resisting Rescuer Role

Holiday get-togethers are fertile ground for volatile family dynamics. I remember wanting to spend one particular Thanksgiving with Artie, my sweetheart. He already had dinner plans, so we intended to get together later. My really close and special girlfriend, Marilyn, and I had discussed having dinner but various relatives and changing commitments halted all that and I was going elsewhere. She invited my sister to join her instead. Then Marilyn got sick, so my sister offered to fix her dinner but, unknown to me, Marilyn declined. When my plans were cancelled at the last minute I called Marilyn and she said, "Well, I'm still sick and really don't know what I want to do. Maybe I'll just stay home, be quiet and have some soup."

Assuming she wanted to be alone I planned to be on my own for Turkey Day joy. But early Thanksgiving afternoon, a wonderful friend from out of town called and we decided to make a holiday dinner together at my place. We had a delightful and companionable early meal. As my friend was leaving, Marilyn called, wondering where I was. She had expected me to bring her dinner and she was hurt. Big misunderstanding! I was so shocked. I searched my memory thinking I must have said something that was misinterpreted. When I suggested bringing some food over now, she said sarcastically, "Don't bother," and hung up. I was shocked. In our many years of friendship, I'd never seen her act toward anyone this way.

I felt the impact of her physical pain shifting into emotional pain and said to my friend, "Boy, she sure is hurting." My guest left and I called Marilyn back. I did not apologize, but said I regretted the mix-up and repeated my offer to come over. She said, "My mother lives closer so I can call her to bring dinner over since now I'm really hungry. I've worked through the feelings of being hurt and am over them, so I need to decide what I want to do."

At first I was confused by her statement, but I began to realize she meant she was going to choose whether to let me or her mother rescue her, and I saw my own choice between rescue and compassion. If I had insisted on rescuing Marilyn, I would not be living my teachings and truths, and would have well and truly bought into guilt and a role as persecutor to her victim (Fear Triad), even though I had done nothing to earn it. So I decided to let Marilyn call her mom and I choose joy and went to Artie's place.

But on the drive to Artie's home, I struggled with feelings of guilt and the urge to "make it better". Despite my innocence in not knowing she expected me to feed her—I felt I had somehow let my friend down. Every few minutes, I'd think, *Well, I could just turn around here and go back and put a little dinner together and take it to her. Then everything would all be all right. I'd have done my duty.* But then it would be a duty, not a joy or something I wanted to do, but just a "should," and based on what? *Guilt* and the fear that she wouldn't love me, that our close friendship of years might not survive this incident. Marilyn had once said she knew I'd always be there for her, so now I felt stuck. I wanted forgiveness. But I knew that forgiveness is never needed because no injury can really *be done to* anyone else. "But why?" I asked myself. Because Marilyn might not love me if I didn't prove to her that I was there for her? Then I woke up.

I suddenly realized I had a choice. I could see my guilt and fear for what they were-that I'd no longer be lovable because I hadn't met someone's expectations. I could choose to continue feeling that way, or I could choose joy in any moment. Hadn't my teacher taught that? Well, I reasoned, if you can't apply those teachings in moments of crisis, then they're just empty words and none of it means anything. But I knew they weren't empty words and that I had to choose to live by them, or I would relapse into old patterns of codependency and guilt by changing my behavior, doing what I didn't want to do, in order to be approved of or feel needed.

It was a tough decision, but I resolved in that moment to walk my talk. I decided to choose joy and allow both Marilyn and myself to be whomever and however we needed to be, and to enjoy the night with Artie.

You may see this as my having chosen my lover over my friend. This was not a choice between them, but **for** me. It was a choice for Self, for beingness, for love of self by self. I saw myself choosing from the triad of Love and moving up out of the triad of Fear. I saw it as a demonstration of the ability to choose joy in any moment, to not make others responsible for my feelings-either guilt or love-and certainly to not make myself responsible for others' feelings. I saw myself as the creator of me in that moment and it was empowering. This was not a choice against, but a choice for.

Even so, driving back from Artie's, I was still doing guilt thinking. Even if all else failed, I rationalized that I would be lovable again because, once Marilyn realized how much I had learned from the "journey," she would be proud of me, shift her blame and hurt, and be pleased at how

I'd handled the "journey." Even this was a plea for her approval and forgiveness. Once I realized what I was doing, I laughed and reminded myself that only I could forgive me. All injuries are done by self to self, knowing that self and other are one. And so I did. I owned all of the experience and let Marilyn own hers. And there it ended.

What a journey we can create, especially if we allow ourselves to experience the full range of feelings involved. We all journey our own feelings within ourselves. Both Marilyn and I grew through this experience. My journey was through guilt. Marilyn's journey was about unlovability, self-responsibility for her own joy, expectations and nurturing issues. By taking the risk of exposing her true feelings when she felt hurt, Marilyn pushed our friendship and our Selves into a new and better awareness. I realize that most friendships are not so metaphysically based. Hopefully, all participants can journey through the full gamut of guilt and blame and come out owning responsibility for their own feelings, honoring the process and being truly thankful for it.

As we talked about it later, Marilyn and I shared our journeys without guilt and blame, in joy and awareness, without ego. There was no striving, no change in caring, no second-guessing, no wondering if punishment would occur, none of the old games and none of the old dynamics. We were still great friends.

When Relationships Die

Whether as friends or lovers, or even in families, relationships last only as long as the need for the experience lasts. When we can no longer grow in self-awareness in a relationship, the true purpose of the union is over. It may remain in place and we may choose to stay in the connection. The length of the relationship is irrelevant. It may have been a whirlwind few days or long term. The beginning of every partnering holds the seeds of its own death. Just as a tree seedling germinates, sprouts, grows, develops, overcomes disease, climate

change, fire and infestation, and ultimately dies, so too does all of
nature, including our relationships. With every new one begins the
long or short journey to its end. Accepting this can be freeing, making
it okay to say goodbye or we can choose fear and hang on for dear life
to the corpse of a dead relationship, which will prevent us from going
on to the next delicious experience. Trusting that there will be another
one is choosing love.

Typically one party recognizes a relationship is over before the
other does. Sometimes we both know it but refuse to take the necessary
steps to dissolve it. Relationships are the arena of our greatest dramas,
our greatest opportunity for victimhood consciousness or self-
empowerment. We get to choose.

Our great fear in ending a relationship is that we won't find another.
As always, fear too is a choice, but not the only one, as the following
story demonstrates.

I had started my relationship with Artie knowing that it wouldn't
be forever because he already had a steady girlfriend. I allowed myself
to fall in love anyway with no expectations at all. I didn't want him for
a permanent mate, but did want to experience all my emotions in a
relationship that didn't have any outcome other than an ending. It was
a wonderful, safe experience, rich and full, though I was always calmly
aware of that inevitable ending.

When Artie had cautioned me about getting hurt, I said, "When
the day comes that we say it's over, I'll meet it with an open heart.
Until then I will not shut down and live in half-shadow, half-experience
or in fear of that happening. I choose to embrace that aspect of our
love, and will walk fearlessly into those feelings, experiencing what it
has to offer. Pain is not to be feared."

In an intimate moment, he again asked, "How will you feel when
I decide that I can no longer continue the relationship?"

That question flipped me into an emotional space I did not want
to be in, of potential pain, of living in the future, and out of the very,

very pleasant now. I chose not to avoid my feelings, but I stayed focused and worked through them, until I discovered what was going on and where my triggers were. I was feeling angry and threatened over his rubbing my nose in my future possible pain and not having any control over it and at unnecessarily having my joy disrupted and being pushed into unpleasantness instead.

I decided to choose love and told him, "Although it seems really weird, I will embrace that time when it comes, even happily, in order to learn and grow from it. I don't want it to occur, but will choose to experience it joyfully, a further part of our relationship.

Why fear anything you haven't yet experienced? I have a choice here, to be in fear or to be in love. Love is a better way to do it. So I'm going to do it consciously."

Having said that, I suddenly realized that the whole issue was actually his guilt over enjoying our intimacy despite being unfaithful to his long-term sweetie. His guilt stemmed from not telling his other lover about us and he was projecting it onto me and I was reacting to it. This is just another form of the rescuer triad wherein he was playing the persecutor, too.

We began discussing this and as I revealed my feelings to him, Artie realized that he was projecting his self-blame. He was amazed that we could process all of this without blame and anger. We were actually enjoying the experience of all that raw emotional vulnerability as part of the journey. This is a part of relationship people miss when they refuse vulnerability.

Knowing that we are in relationships for the expression and development of Self lets us stay present and look freely at our own issues, free of ego defenses. Choosing to give to Self out of Love leads us to these personal insights. This is what it means to be centered in Self. Relationships truly are about each person, not "us," nor the relationship, but about Self.

Betrayal in Friendship

Just as romantic relationships carry the seeds of their death, so too do friendships. Some just fade away as people move or choose different lifestyles. Some go out in fiery flames of anger, hurt or jealousy. Some remain co-dependent and others writhe in the twists and turns of constant change in on again-off again affairs.

Relationships serve us until they don't. Sometimes one party recognizes this before the other does. Sometimes we know the relationship is over but refuse to take the necessary steps to dissolve it. Relationships are the arena of our greatest dramas, our greatest opportunity for victim-hood consciousness or for self-empowerment. We get to choose.

Acquaintances come and go in our lives. We are fortunate indeed if we can name five people as true friends. Friendship is a good place to act out the play of Triadic Creation of Love or Fear. We have a tendency to be a little more authentic in our friendships because we do not have sexual favors as the prize or weapon.

I have always been shocked by betrayal in a friendship and found the pain hard to deal with. After several experiences, I had to look at why I was repeatedly creating betrayal in my life. I did not want to continue to manifest such unhealthy situations over and over, but was lost. I had to know why. I felt like a victim but I could use the triangles as the perfect key to understanding how I was creating.

My first step was to decide to stop focusing on the hurt. Then I had to choose to forgive. We need to use forgiveness as a baby step until we learn that there is no real need for it. Forgiving the other person was often too difficult, so I had to begin with forgiving me and loving myself. I knew I was playing the victim here. I was making the other person into a persecutor. I knew I had the tools to figure this out, so I asked myself, "Since anything that is not loving is fear based, what is the fear?" Then I asked, "How does it serve me to continue to bring betrayal into my life? Where is the payoff?"

Since fear of lack of control has always been my main issue, I realized that I was manifesting friendships that had the same issues. I also realized I had some blind spots in my friendships, notably my refusal to see the shadow side of someone's nature. When we do this, we have surely overlooked our own. By "shadow side," I mean the darker elements, the hidden ones that bite, such as denial, greed, backbiting, gossip, pilfering, pretense, judgment, and envy. To some degree, we all have these aspects within us. For some of us, the intensity of such a negative trait is negligible, but for others it consumes the personality. By being willing to recognize and accept all the traits of our personalities as part of our humanity, we can begin to disarm and embrace them one by one until they are a "no thing."

To illustrate, if we are asked to take the garbage out, we must first acknowledge its existence, then choose to remove it, and finally take hold of it in order to move it. The point is we cannot get rid of something until we first acknowledge its existence and then take hold of it. Denial gets us nowhere and prevents us from growing.

I realized that if I became aware of all the other person's faults, they might see all of mine and I wouldn't be lovable. If I overlooked their faults, they'd have to overlook mine. But they didn't. They could see me anyway. In another bold attempt at self-misdirection, I refused to see jealousy. I thought friends were supposed to look past each other's faults as well as their gifts, and not feel jealous. But all the while, they were becoming victims of their own lack of self-worth and growing jealous of my accomplishments. So they sabotaged the relationship to avoid falling short in their own eyes. Discovering this took me years. This, too, was part of my control issues.

My first clue about how this worked came one day when my closest friend told me that, as a teenager, she'd struggled through many years of piano lessons and could finally play a particular piece. On hearing her play it, her sister, who'd studied piano for only a year, sat down and played the whole thing flawlessly. Outdone, demoralized, and totally jealous, my friend never touched the piano again. She had huge self-worth issues; her sister had become her persecutor and she the victim. Instead of pride in her own accomplishments, she chose jealousy. Instead of love of self, she chose lack of self-worth. Though I knew her severely abusive background contributed to her belief systems and choices. I thought she'd gotten past that but was proven wrong.

Another shock was betrayal by Marilyn (whom we met in the previous chapter). I had manifested a wonderful friendship with her and learned how to be more available to my female energy, allowing, nurturing, intuitive and open. But I ended up standing more in her power and dealing with her lack of self-worth. I had thought we would have a lifetime friendship but after seven years it was over. It had accomplished its reason for being. To cling to it would have been disempowering, co-dependent and suffocating. We were growing in different directions and that growth required space.

Not seeing the need for new growth approaching resulted in the destructive dissolution of that friendship. I know close friends and family are the safest to be the angriest with, but Marilyn took anger to new heights. She verbally attacked me one day for several hours and I was thoroughly destroyed emotionally. I definitely felt I was a victim and knew I needed help immediately. I stayed in my feelings, connected with the highest god-like aspect of myself and manifested a counselor to help me. I was broken and the counselor, whom I knew, would be my rescuer.

I told her, "Such a good friend as Marilyn has to be right and would never attack me without cause. I need to find out where I was wrong, and fix myself. I'm open to hearing all the bad things about me."

She listened carefully to the whole story and then calmly told me, "This is one of the most blatant cases of verbal abuse I've ever heard. All the things Marilyn said to you were her own issues projected on to you."

Needless to say, I was stunned. I was prepared to hear anything but that. My self-worth was at an all-time low, but just those few sentences changed all that. The counselor did not do guilt and blame. She just stated the facts. She was not rescuing or creating another victim. She was plainly describing what was in front of her. With the help of this counselor I went through some intense resolution of my anger towards Marilyn. I beat a punching bag with a rubber hose, something I recommend for anyone to get in touch with and to transmute their anger.

I knew I had moved past victimhood when, at the end of the session, the counselor suggested another appointment and refused to take any more money saying, "Your friendship is worth more to me than money."

I was validated for being me. I wasn't the disgusting, horrid person Marilyn had claimed I was. When I arrived home, I received several calls from near and far away friends just calling to say hello. Some I hadn't heard from in months. None of them had known about any of my experience involving Marilyn, so they weren't rescuing me. It was just love being manifested. I no longer felt like a victim. I'd run the gauntlet and had come through just fine.

There's much more to relationships than we realize. When they have achieved their purpose, they are over. With gratitude in your heart, give them a decent burial, move through the grief process and get on with your life.

Authority Figures: The Landlord From Hell

I was in the home my mate and I had rented with option to purchase when, during a snowstorm, our landlord suddenly arrived, knocked on our door and went berserk about our not weeding the yard. His brother was with him and we reminded him that in negotiating our lease, he had specifically said, "You are not to do the yard. My brother will."

We couldn't understand why he was so crazed. The weeds he saw— all sixteen of them—were inaccessible in the snow. Obsessed, he and his brother followed us into the house where he told us, "I'm the landlord. You're only the tenant. It's my house, not yours."

He returned at Christmas and again made an issue about the weeds. He wanted to start an argument but my sweetheart was on the phone learning his sister had cancer. Overloaded and angry, he told them to leave, closed the door on them and went back to the phone call. Now both my sweetheart and the landlord were really ticked off. The next day, the landlord was back, making threats and demanding we park both of our cars in the garage where only one would fit.

On New Year's Day, things got decidedly worse. The landlord phoned to demand entry to repair code violations to the smoke detectors we had been requesting for some time.

It would have been easy to see the landlord as our persecutor, but I was determined not to play a victim role. Instead, I tried to figure out *why we had created this experience.* By 10 a.m., the morning he was due, I was anticipating conflict and my stomach was one huge knot. Fortunately, I was not attached to becoming the owner of the house, which was a good start. The possibility of being evicted and having to move was depressing, but I figured that the universe must have one incredible place in mind for us. We decided to just stay in the flow, and allow it all.

Instead of anger and judgment I wanted to consciously choose who and what I AM when they arrived that morning. So I choose to be love. But how do I do that in this situation? How do I move past my fear before they get here?"

I picked up a book opening it to a page I'd marked. I read: *Love is unlimited and freeing.* That was just the reminder I needed. I allowed myself to feel unlimited and free, to claim becoming love as mine. An hour later, I went downstairs, found my front door open and the landlord and his brother already inside the house!

In that moment, I knew I could choose to be angry at this violation and illegal trespass, or to just be grateful the repairs would now be done. "The situation is in hand and can be dealt with," I told myself. "I choose to be open, vulnerable, loving and allow the trespass, but will let them know that they have trespassed." So I asked, "Did you ring the bell?"

"Yes," they said.

"Oh, I didn't hear you," I replied, and left it at that, though I felt violated. It was opportunity #2 to choose victim and fear, or love and allowance. I chose the latter. They fixed the smoke detectors, replaced the battery and we went upstairs.

Because I had chosen love, I was calm, happy and open, with no resentment, hostility or holding back. No expectations, just being. Then I remembered a joke about the Energizer Bunny and a battery, and told it to them. One brother laughed; they were beginning to loosen up. He was beginning to be normal, not so angry and threatening any more. Soon they were talking evenly, coming to balance with my requests and my ease of being. Since I wasn't putting out fear-based vibrations, they didn't have to hold onto resistance. Then the landlord said, "I'm glad we're back on track with our relationship."

I said, "Yes, my partner was overloaded when he yelled at you before and wants to apologize. Please accept his apologies."

They were laughing by then. We discussed the list of our 'violations' and he said, "Don't worry about it. I was reacting to your partner's anger and everything got out of control."

Then he said something about his conduct that I knew was an obvious lie, and I had opportunity #3 to choose between fear and love. I chose love. By then it was easy.

I began writing the rent check and he said "Why don't you make it $50 less and buy yourself a new light fixture to replace the one that's causing you problems?"

"How sweet of you," I said, and really meant it. In essence, the whole eruption had been transmuted from fear to love. I wanted to *be* only love and to *be* fearless. My choosing to be love had disarmed a bomb that had threatened to blow up in our faces. We did eventually purchase our lovely home.

The Workplace

Dealings with authority figures at work can be just as difficult and painful. The workplace scenario is full of victims, persecutors and rescuers. Do we continually see bosses, employees and co-workers in our thoughts as tyrants or can we see them as fearful children? Running a business or being a manager in a company is stressful and allows for much fear-based conduct.

In your own situation, can you learn to operate within the Love triangle? Can you learn how to give these 'children in adult bodies' the reinforcement they so desperately need in order to allay their fears? Can you tell your controlling boss that he is good at something? Yes, you can do these things. Most likely, your boss is desperately seeking approval and uses bullying, faultfinding and criticism to make himself feel important and validated. So validate him. Be honest and sincere. Tell him his job is important and that you appreciate his position. That may be all he's looking for.

A client once told me she was considering quitting her job because of her boss and asked me how to deal with him. I asked her, "Have you ever complimented him on the job he's doing?"

"No way!" she exclaimed.

"Well, I suggest that you find something about him to appreciate, to compliment or validate. But you must be sincere. The compliment must flow naturally and not be just injected into conversation. You'll have an interesting time feeling your own shift at trying to find something to compliment your boss about. You'll begin to see ways to look for the good in someone. You'll come to realize how much you've been focused on the negative."

Relationships are certainly not limited to romance or close friends. You can certainly draw many revealing stories from your own experiences with parents, church leaders, police, teachers, bankers, neighbors, family, bureaucrats, courts and many others.

As we've already learned, what you focus on, you get more of. You elicit from others the very qualities in them that you focus on. So shift your focus! Find ways to validate, include, and approve of your coworkers, boss and employees. You will shift the whole dynamics of your work place. Unlock your own hurt feelings and fears, and shift your own attitude. But before looking for the good in others, begin looking for it within yourself. After all, you and others are in fact One.

Chapter 10

Why We Have Money Problems

We've learned so well to be limited, to stay "inside the box." In the famous diagram below, the object is to draw four straight lines that pass through all nine dots without removing the pen from the paper. (Hint: you will not be able to do this with limited thinking.) You must go "outside the box." No one said you couldn't. It is simply that your mind struggles, perceiving limitation within the mentally imposed edges of the box. Remember, *argue for your limitations and you get to keep them*. Try it here for yourself. You will find the solution on page 188.

Our mind is a huge asset as well as one of our greatest impediments, urging us to stay inside beliefs and limited thinking. It tricks us into the "Yes, but" syndrome. Yes, I could achieve wealth but it's too much work. Yes, I want a better job, but I'm scared of rejection. Yes, there's got to be a better way, but gosh, it's too much work.

In order to get out of your own way and see outside of the 9 dots. you can get counseling, read books and meditate, paying attention to how you're thinking. Take notice of how you react to topics concerning money. Are you angry and resentful when you pay your bills? Try appreciating your money. Be pleased you have enjoyed the benefit of the product or service and that you have the wealth to pay for it. Yes, wealth. You're still going to pay them. It's just the attitude you bring to the effort that will make a difference. The more you focus on outgo and the fear of "not enough," the more "not enough" you bring to you. Shift your thinking from negative focus to positive, lack to abundance. Only you stand in your way.

Remember when you first graduated from school and felt invincible, and the whole world was your oyster? You had a degree and you just knew you could do anything! You had basically nothing but attitude, potential and positive outlook. Where did these assets go? Nowhere. They're still there if you will but take them out of your pocket, out of your closet and out of your heart. Sure, life's bumps and bruises may have put a dent in your rosy outlook but you can still have one, tempered, and full of the yet to be experienced. You get to decide if life is *for* you or *against* you. When you make your decision, you will either be standing in your own way or standing in your own potential.

This is how you create that abundance mindset that actually brings money to you. Focus on wealth and its abundance or on poverty and its inherent fear of lack. What you focus on you get more of.

You get to choose.

Abundance is our natural God-given state. The universe is perfectly abundant. God didn't create lack. Any sense of deficiency we have is from shutting off our internal valves to wealth and our ability to receive. We may be born into a life that has a consciousness of poverty, a contagious thinking and feeling. Or we may have been born with a silver spoon in our mouth and a prevailing family consciousness is that the world is ours and we have but to pluck abundance from it. We can take only a thimble full of abundance or several semi-trucks loads. It's up to us. It is an attitude, a given, an emotional state. Our attitudes and feelings about wealth determine our ability to create it on the physical plane. The universe has enough for everyone, total and complete abundance! Each of us can have all the wealth we desire. The key is our desire and the passion to have what we prefer. But if our peers, culture or the group we were born into have programmed us to believe in limitation, we must break out of that limitation first.

On the way to wealth, many changes occur that may deter us. Friends may become jealous. Parents may think you're better than them. Peers may want to keep you in their own comfort zone. Any disturbance of the status quo threatens those close to the passionate seeker of wealth, change, growth or spirituality. When one of our friends breaks the shell of these restricting patterns and blossoms before our eyes, we are easily threatened by our fear that we may not be living up to our potential. In addition, fear of losing this support system may stop us in our tracks.

Fear of financial lack can be so overwhelming that we stay in school, relationships, jobs and cities far too long. We fear making it on our own. We've heard too many horror stories of loss and failure. We've bought into the ideas, fears, limitations and belief systems of our family, neighbors, co-workers, teachers and the media. We must look at where we learned all our ideas about money. Do those belief systems still serve us? Are they outdated? Are they just based on fears? There are many success stories we can choose to focus upon.

My parents were raised in the depression of the 1930s, which gave them a poverty consciousness that required saving scraps of odds and ends in case one day we needed them. When shopping, they were lookers, not buyers. They were taught us to ask, "Do I *really* need this?" before buying something. They saved. They had learned to do with less, to buy in quantity and stock up, to can their own produce. We lived by phrases like "A penny saved is a penny earned," "Don't count your chickens before they're hatched," "Look, don't touch," "Check prices in other stores before you buy," and "Wait for a sale." It was shameful to waste, to overspend or to risk. These were healthy ideas for the 1930s. But they do not reflect the 1980s or 1990s or the new millennium. If my sisters and I had chosen never to risk, we'd have lived lives very similar to theirs, which we definitely didn't want to do.

Breaking out of these thinking patterns took a while, but I did it, little by little. I was the first to go to college, so was expected to make more of myself than my parents had. I was also taught that I could do anything I set my mind to and with this attitude I could accomplished my heart's desires.

We get to choose how we apply the guidance of our mentors, parents and teachers. Do we choose to be limited by them or take the ones that reinforce us and run with them? It's a choice. We are either victims of those teachings or creators of our own experiences. What we think, we can do. We can "think outside the box."

Solution

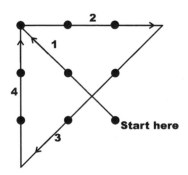

Breaking Free

One way to break out of the old money teachings and belief systems is to make a list of what you think about wealth and rich people. Ask yourself what tapes you are playing about wealth:

- Do you believe wealth and spirituality are incompatible?
- Do you believe that your parents knew best about money and work?
- Do you believe that there isn't enough money for everyone in the world; that if you get rich, others will be wanting?
- Do you believe that if you become wealthy you'd lose your friends?
- Do you believe that since your parents never had any money, you shouldn't either?
- Do you believe that money would make you seem better than your friends?
- Do you believe that people who have money probably obtained it illegally, underhandedly or by hurting others?
- Do you believe that all rich people cheated to become successful?
- Do you believe money is evil?
- Do you believe prosperity would create too many headaches, perhaps tax problems, uncertainty about new decisions and other people hounding you?
- Do you believe that rich people take advantage of others?

Make a list of "what ifs" about being wealthy:

- What would be your feelings towards self, possessions, family or friends?
- What would you do if you won $5,000,000 in the Lotto?
- What would you do with money if you were Bill Gates? Spend it? Save it? Give it away? Invest it?
- What would be your attitudes about making that much money, about being gifted with that much money?
- How would your life be different?

Just write down your thoughts and feelings as you read these questions. Let it flow. Don't judge anything that comes to you. You'll be astonished at the secret fears, belief systems and old tapes that you unlock. Whose tapes are they? Do they serve you any longer? Do you want to change them? How can you change them?

Feel Your Abundance

A secret key to wealth is to touch into the feeling tones of your attitudes and emotions about not only money, but the making of it and the dealing with it, holding it, keeping it, using it, spending it and even losing it. Each of these aspects about money pushes emotional triggers which, once uncovered, may help resolve why you manifest lack, and hold off receiving your universal inheritance of wealth, be it physical, health-wise, or whatever. Focus on where you are already abundant and feel that abundance.

Not having enough or having too much of anything, the issues are the same—*fear*, plain and simple. Let's look at those five fears again:

- Fear of Unlovability
- Fear of Lack of Self Worth
- Fear of Lack
- Fear of Lack of Control
- Fear of Separation

It's pretty clear that all five fears are operative with money situations, even when you have huge amounts of it. (A superb workbook on this subject is *Consciously Creating Wealth* by Cody Horton.)

Hanging Out With the Wealthy

Another way to break free is to hang out with the wealthy at yacht clubs, fancy restaurants, country clubs, racetrack stables, or even gourmet shops. You'll begin to experience a different mindset and attitude. Some of it you may not like. That's fine. Choose what you do like. Reading books about famous wealthy people will help you see how it is their attitudes that make the difference. Adopt their gift of vision, their creativity and their fearlessness.

Realistic Affirmations

Affirmations are those wonderful sayings that people stick up on their mirrors, their desks, their walls and in their cars. They say things such as, "I am happy," "I am rich," and "I am beautiful." These are great messages to send to the subconscious. But if the subconscious doesn't believe them, then they are reinforcements of what you DO NOT have. The subconscious responds, "Horse Pucky! I'm not pretty, I'm not rich, I can barely pay my bills, and I'm depressed and angry!" Affirmations only work when they state what your body already agrees with. Use them, but change them.

Suppose you want to lose weight. Say, "I am willing to give up my addiction to food." If you react and think/feel, *but I like my greasy hamburgers*, then your body won't align with the affirmation and it's all an exercise in ego. If that affirmation isn't *real* to your body, then say, "I am willing to *look at* giving up my addiction to food."

"Ahhhhhh," the body responds. "Yes, we can do that! It's not so threatening."

You have moved mountains this way. Your body begins to align with a willingness to shift. Later you can choose one of the other affirmations and move closer to your desire.

If you have a problem making money, ask yourself, " How am I receiving from myself?" That is the issue. If you cannot receive from self, you can't receive from the universe. When you deny the self, you create lack outside yourself. Begin to give to self, unlimitedly. Ask, "How can I create happiness in this moment?" and have the wisdom to choose whatever it is. Go to that creative power within you and give to self in this moment. Would you like a drink of water in this now? Would you like to take a nap? Would you like to go for a walk? What are you not asking for yourself *right now*? This is the beginning of honoring the Self. Material abundance is a manifestation of what was first intended ... then believed ... then accepted as completely real, as real-ized. If you doubt this, read my story Chapter I of how a young couple became millionaires and wound up bankrupt. Thought plus emotion creates.

Why I Went Bankrupt

I didn't understand the true reasons why I lost it all until years afterward.

First, I wasn't in joy and therefore, no longer on my path. The workload had become burdensome. It was a case of the tail wagging the dog. The hours were brutal, the demands endless. We had begun purchasing property in 1972 when it made economic sense and we were building a future. It was fun. Second, we had assembled a good crew and suddenly, we felt responsible for their continued employment. Thus a subtle change occurred. We began to buy fixers *for them*. We had switched to being rescuers. But it didn't stop there. Third, at some point we crossed over a line of self-worth. *We had exceeded our limits of how big we'd ever have imagined we'd become.* Fourth, in order to justify it all, we began providing housing for drug and alcohol abusers. It seemed like a good idea. Then we set up housing for abused women. That was a good idea, too. But by now we were well on the path of rescuing lots of others. When you play in the victim triangle, you are participating in all the parts of it. Eventually, the tables will turn and you will become a victim, well and truly operating from the Fear Triad.

I began to plan how to provide jobs, training and child care for the low income families of the area. I was so far into the rescue experience that I had lost total view of the joy of our original path. It was all becoming "should's," "have to's" and social responsibility.

Many of you will say, "Well, what's wrong with that? It's noble, honorable, and someone should do it."

Hmm, that sounds an awful lot like a "should." You see, by setting up a rescue business, I had bought into fear. In rescuing, I was dishonoring the choices and godhood of each individual I helped. I was actually contributing to the victim-hood consciousness of the neighborhood by defining and reinforcing so many others as victims. I was not honoring their journey. Subconsciously I had lost the direction of my original intent when purchasing property. *I had reached the limit of my subconscious self-worth.* Fearing exposure that I wasn't as good as I thought I was, I sought moral justification for continual acquisition. Fear of lack of self-worth became the real driving force. Then fear of lack, of running out of funds, became the impetus to purchase more and more properties because the net proceeds of the purchase loans where needed to keep the business going.

I am not saying that all help programs are flawed as rescuers, but many, many are. Everything depends on the intent. Most intentions seem grand and excellent, but are based on the rescue of victims. At the very least they are a helping hand, a "hand out," which says, "I know your path better than you do. I am judging the path you have chosen as bad, less than, or in need of fixing. Therefore you are broken, incapable of choosing for yourself, and your experience as a creator of your own life is in question."

Excuse me? No one is broken. Each one's path is perfect just as they have chosen it. No one is to be judged, no matter how "flawed" they may appear. Each one of us is always standing in his or her Godhood. We may need reminding at times that we are creators and aspects of God. We ultimately want to be empowered, not dis-empowered. My fears actually caused the disempowerment of many. I was unconscious of it at the time, and it has literally taken many years to understand why and how my empire really collapsed.

We are open to receive when we revere *all* of life, when we love ourselves and see that we are worthy of receiving. I had moved beyond the ability to see my self-worth. I had exceeded it and now had to justify it. And as day follows night, my creations began to reflect that change. They began to be based on Victim, Persecutor and Rescuer. Out of this fear, all my creative results changed direction and reflected those unhealthy dynamics. I could not stop its great momentum because I was still "asleep." I became enmeshed in its snare, a victim myself. At that point, however, I chose to become conscious of my situation and not play the victim role. Although rescuers in the guise of attorneys offered me such a choice later, I was then awake enough to recognize the game and said no.

For one's highest work to continue, each must retain the vision of wholeness and perfection in others, in each moment. What an awesome challenge. The Rescue business can be such an enticing trap.

Reprogramming Our Feelings

Our operating system is programmed by emotionally impacting experiences. To change how it operates, we can consciously give it new emotional experiences that align with what we prefer to experience in our life. Since thought plus emotions create, use the mind to choose which feelings we desire. Then use our emotional self to feel them. It is the combination that produces the results. As described earlier, once you've brought up these new positive feelings about what you want, feel them. Focus on them, over and over, remembering to stay with them at least 17 seconds each time. The longer you maintain focus, the more impact the focus has. Your subconscious will get the new message and begin creating accordingly and you will find yourself creating from the Love Triad.

Once you've created the experience, you must also let go of it. Do not keep worrying about it to see if it's happened. This is like planting a seed and, instead of just allowing it to grow, you keep digging it up to see if it's germinated.

Years ago I attended a seminar that taught this manifestation principle, of letting go, at a retreat center near Mt Rainier. I had become highly upset and emotional about my financial predicament. As we drove to dinner through the woods, my companion said he wondered if we'd see any wild elk. I took it as a challenge to manifest elk, but not just one or two way off in the distance, I wanted to see a lot of them up close so there was no doubt it was a real experience. In my overwrought state I demanded the universe show us some elk. Then I let go of the need to have it happen. I knew that my thoughts and intensity of emotion would insure its happening. Within two minutes we saw one elk, then two and finally had to stop the car to let a herd of over 75 cross the mountain highway in front of our car, no less than 50 feet away. I remember the emotional state of demand, letting go, allowance and the knowing that produced such striking results.

Since that time, I have called forth, demanded, ordered the universe to find me an apartment (that took a few hours), an airplane flight (that took less than an hour) and other practical items. The keys seem to be 1) originating thought, 2) passion, 3) releasing the need for outcome and 4) knowing you and the universe are inseparable.

When you align with universal abundance, know that you are the creator expression of God. Trust in the Universe and create from an emotional space of love, combining thought with that emotion, and your creations will be in alignment with your highest and best good. Your creations will be in joy. You cannot be a victim. You will have achieved an inner peace as the source of Love.

You Get What You Ask For

When I started working, I had inherited that old work ethic that says, "You must work hard to make a living. If you put in a solid eight, maybe nine hours a day, every day, you'll be fine."

Fine is a matter of perspective. You may be familiar with this particular fairy tale. After living this way for many years, you wake up and realize that it was a fable, but the world doesn't need to work that way. When I finally woke up, I decided I'd like to create abundance in short, but happy, concentrated work periods that would leave me lots of free time. So I created such an experience. By this time I was doing readings so I alternated intense, profitable psychic fairs with minimal work or nothing at all. In the beginning, having forgotten that I'd put such an order in to the universe, I'd panic. "What if I don't get any more readings? I won't be able to pay the rent."

After several cycles of work, no work, joy, then panic, I remembered my Universal Order: lots of free time and concentrated work periods. I clung to it, knowing that I was manifesting exactly what I'd ordered. Finally, I stopped freaking out at every dormant period realizing that I'd asked for lots of free time so I could play a lot. I'd call a friend in California and fly down to have fun for a couple of weeks. Magically, when I returned, the recorder was full of requests for appointments. It became a game. Go play and be in joy. Let the answering machine collect all that joyous energy in the form of business so that you can be in joy all the time. The amount of work available to me on my return from these mini-vacations was in direct proportion to the level of joy I'd created while I was gone. In other words, *the greater the fear, the less the work; the greater the joy, the more the work.*

I learned that if I stayed in the flow, focused on and actually chose joy, then I was in alignment with the universal flow. In that space, abundance comes naturally because this is an abundant universe. It was only when I stopped the flow and fell out of alignment with my knowing that the Universe and I were One, that I turned off the tap to my abundance.

Often when I did the large international fairs, I received magnificent lessons and made huge leaps in personal growth, including with my money issues. I'd always made good money there and soon began looking forward to the personal growth side of the experience and downplayed the income side, as though growth were a higher priority. My expenses were just barely paid and I made little profit. This taught me they are equal priorities. We need not suffer lack in order to obtain spiritual growth. That is part of the old paradigm that we must have pain in order to have gain. This was never true. The belief that spirituality and money are opposites is blatantly false.

In one particular fair, the lights above my booth were out, so I was pretty much in the dark and at the end of an aisle in a low-traffic location. I knew I created my own reality and wondered what was going on. Then all the lights in the entire exhibition hall actually went out, so we figured there was a "power" problem and we worked with clients in the semi-dark.

I had also finally learned not to "sell" my consultations but to just let people come to me. I was using more feminine energy this way, becoming more magnetic. I learned by watching others. I would just allow, know and trust that the right people would come to me. I closed my eyes and visualized a garden path to my booth so that there was a feel to it for those of like energy to follow. I visualized my booth as a charming cottage, with coffee freshly brewed, window boxes with flowers, cozy, sacred, safe and private within, where the weary traveler could find rest, peace and insights. Immediately upon opening my eyes, two clients were already standing at my booth and I began to do readings. I did not stop until closing time. To top it off, the lights directly over my booth went out again the second morning. My booth appeared dark, with no light to draw people to me. I instantly changed it to an asset by visualizing a dark cave that offered privacy. The dim lighting would attract clients wanting that experience. It worked. I gave several readings before the light was even fixed. The point here is that if I'd wanted to experience lack, I could have flowed my energy towards being the victim, angry about the lighting, making someone guilty and demanding the light be fixed. Instead, I owned being the creator of my reality and used what was there, changing it to my advantage. It is all in the perception. It's just a choice.

A Wealth of Symbols; a Symbol of Wealth

Those on the journey inward who have discovered internal wealth know it to be true wealth. They no longer participate in the consciousness that seeks external wealth through accumulation. They no longer depend on or seek to accrue "things" outside the body as symbols, such as cars, clothes or jewelry that we mistake for wealth. Having achieved a sense of real prosperity, they stop feeling it necessary to manifest external wealth because it is manifested internally. This does not mean they are poor or have shabby belongings. It means they are not so attached to the accumulation, display and preservation of objects. They are no longer crippled by society's belief that they should appear in a particular way. If they do not meet society's requirements, they no longer fear unlovability for they no longer need approval of who they are.

In taking baby steps to creating abundance, we need to bridge the gap between feeling wealth within and having it appear outside of us, in our reality. We can do this by going inside to find a personal symbol of that internal wealth that we can make in tangible, three-dimensional, form we can look at and touch. When you hold it in your hand, externalized, *real*-ized, you have concretized your physical wealth on the outside. Having a physical representation of your wealth allows your subconscious to know that abundance is real for you. It demonstrates the ancient axiom: As above, so below; as within, so without.

When you go inside to discover your wealth symbol, do so from a reflective or meditative state. Become relaxed and peaceful. Allow your mind to focus on wealth and let your imagination bring forth a symbol. You may receive it on your first, second or even third try. When I did this exercise, I found the image of a lotus. I had always loved this beautiful flower image and still use it in my logo, but it was still un-real-ized, not yet made real in a three-dimensional way. It remained a background thing, flat and two-dimensional. I was unaware that it had been my expression of wealth within me all along.

Prior to this exercise a good friend had given me a charming lotus candle, two inches tall and four inches wide, with gorgeous pink petals and yellow center. Too lovely to burn, it rested in a special place in my home. When I received the lotus image as my symbol of wealth, I suddenly became aware that my decision to save the candle was just like my issue with abundance. The candle was created for burning, to be useful, beautiful and shed light. It wasn't meant to be stored up, saved and admired forever. We must use it to experience its purpose. As with abundance, I was saving my funds. Money is just energy and is meant to be circulated and used. If we store it up endlessly for fear of lack, we do ourselves a disservice. We get stuck. Our money gets stuck. Our ability to receive money and stay in the flow is adversely affected. I had stopped the flow so I burned the candle and freed my locked up ideas about money, locked up in that unburned candle that represented abundance to me. I'd finally gotten it. *Money isn't meant to be stored up. There will always be enough.*

Wealth is like air, always plentiful. If we align ourselves with the knowing that the universe is perfectly abundant, then we have access to it when we need it. But it is not stored in piles. It is fully available upon tapping into the never-ending flow. We don't fear lack of air. We know it is always there. So is abundance, if we would *know* it. Only when we block its flow, through our fear of its lack, do we create the very lack we fear.

We manifest wealth by learning what is blocking us and discovering healthier ways to meet those fears. We manifest wealth by our emotions coupled with our thoughts about money. If you have money issues, look deeply at your beliefs about wealth and wealthy people, for that is where the blockage lies.

Being Given Money

Receiving money can be as difficult as not having enough. Many independent women have difficulty with stopping or ending their careers when a child comes along. The idea that they now must be supported is a shock to their self-worth. They have become victims of receiving abundance. Likewise, recipients of a family inheritance often feel guilt at becoming wealthy from the death of another. The trap here is valuing yourself according to what you *do*, not who you *are*. It is based on low self-worth and the belief that if you did not have to work hard for something, it has no real value. Open yourself to receive. You are already worth it.

Money versus God

Once when I was seeing clients in Canada, a man came to see me who said, "I am the chief and spiritual leader of a large group of Native Americans. I am concerned about a great choice facing me. I have the opportunity to accept a government contract that would create employment for 300 of my people, but I would have to oversee the job. It concerns me that I would have to set my spirituality aside to go into the contracting business."

For him, it was an either-or situation. He believed that money and Spirit were separate. Since he was the leader of his people, he felt responsible for both their spiritual and physical welfare. Since he greatly valued his spiritual focus, he could not reconcile money and Creator. He did not know how to choose.

I reminded him, "Nothing exists that is not Spirit. Everything is already connected through Creator and is already One. Do you believe that Creator, Great Spirit, God is everywhere?"

"Yes," he replied.

I then asked him, "Do you believe that God created everything?" Again he responded, "Yes."

"Then why would you believe money was not an aspect of the Creator and just as spiritual as anything else? There is no need to choose between the two. They are inseparable. Everything is energy vibrating at a different rate. Everything is spiritual. So is money."

His face lit up. His shoulders relaxed. He had found "the path between", a third option, and recognized his solution.

So often we believe that we must choose between two things. In truth, we can also choose what lies between two things, a resolution, an in-between, a blending. Look for a third alternative when facing either-or choices. It makes life easier.

Remember, we are not physical beings having a few spiritual experiences. We are spiritual beings having a few physical experiences. Everything we could possibly think of to do or to be is an expression of that energy, sheathed in the illusion of form and structure.

Most of us have issues with abundance. Often we believe God and money are at opposite ends of the spiritual spectrum. However, the one is simply an aspect in the other. It is how it is applied, experienced and used that makes the difference. Remember, energy is neither good nor bad. It's what we do with it that makes the difference.

Nothing is truly evil, but our thinking that makes it so.

Chapter 11

Crisis, Great and Small

All crises are relevant in their impact on us. It may be surprising to learn that studies show when group members discusses their personal crisis, in the final analysis, each participant agrees they would prefer their own crisis to that of others. It seems that no matter how terrible, crisis is very personal. It shapes us. We align with it. We become changed by its impact. In my practice, I hear of many horrific experiences. The higher part of us, the part that remembers its connection with God, steers us through trauma. It knows why we experience crisis and why we created it in our world. It judges not. It sees clearly how such an event serves the individual and mankind as a whole. As you read through this chapter, keep in mind that withholding judgment allows an event's spiritual purpose to be revealed to us. By staying in the flow of non-judgment, our thoughts and emotions align with our higher knowing.

Emotions in Crisis

At no time will emotions cease for us. We will always continue to feel. As we grow spiritually, our reactions to those emotions will even out, become less and less volatile and reactive. Mastery is becoming predictable in the calmness of your reactions. When you find yourself reactive and emotional, you are having feelings. Allow them. Acknowledge them. Ask yourself if you want to express those emotions at that time. It may or may not be advisable in that moment. For instance, with anger, you may be unable to express it because you are holding a baby, or in a hospital room with someone ill. If so, acknowledge your anger in that moment, even if only to yourself. Be sure to give vent to them later, in a healthy manner. Then, you may wish to take a rubber hose and repeatedly strike a tree stump. In Japan they have rooms full of mockups of expensive vases and furniture that you pay to smash. Early Native Americans dug a hole in the earth, screamed and vomited their anger into the hole and then planted a seed there to honor the transmutation of the anger into a plant's growth.

I'm Only Doing My Job

Beth was on floor duty at the real estate office. That meant it was her day to see to all the walk-in or phone-in business. A man entered the office and subsequently negotiated a purchase that led to a series of events ending with Beth filing bankruptcy, losing her house and then later, her job. In telling her story, she would say, "I was just on floor duty." In full victimhood she denied any sense of having created or even co-created that experience.

Beth had a history of victimhood consciousness stemming from her mother's treatment of her. From early childhood, this behavior and thinking was reinforced. Everyone else had control in her life, and they always abused her. Her marriages failed, her boss was difficult and demanding. Her church leader had an affair with her and then dumped her. Always she was the victim. In fact, if it weren't for bad luck, she would have no luck at all! When she is ready, Beth will make a choice for herself to wake up and stop being a victim…or not. The universe will completely support her in all her choices. It is her path. When her conduct ceases having a payoff or it becomes too painful to remain in her victim role, she will be motivated to shift. Perhaps she will choose joy. It's always a choice.

Payoff for Victims and Thrashers

If Beth would allow herself to take a deep breath and step back to look at her life, she would recognize she constantly creates her life around drama. People thrash around (flailing in the sea of busyness, doingness, limitation and fear) in their lives because there is some sort of payoff. It may be attention, feeling alive, or self-hatred. Most people do not live in such an extreme way, but many, many do. Why?

Take the abused woman. Why does she create a new abuser in her life after finally getting away from the old one? How does she find them? What does she have in common with Beth? Victim consciousness. You get more of what you focus on. To create such trauma over and over, one must be soaked in fears. Somehow it continues to serve the person.

How do you extricate yourself and change the outcomes? By owning that you create these experiences, and that not everyone else is having them. By seeing that there is a different way to create that has far better results. By recognizing how these dramas are creating your chosen payoff in your life, you can begin to create differently.

Stepping Into Your Power

You must first see yourself as powerful in your current creations. Know it. Own it. Feel it. Bravo! Hats off to you! Hurrah! You have done it perfectly. You are waking up. You are beginning to look at other choices and deciding that you want a different outcome.

Here is where most of us are stuck. We do not know how to go about making such changes as letting go of the old payoffs. We do not know what steps to take to get to a new perspective, a new place. We look elsewhere, take classes, seek gurus, but it never sticks. Because there is really no other place to go, the only place to make changes is within. Expand who you are, including more and more understanding and enlightenment, until you are finally awake.

This is the journey to self. This is living authentically. Of course the simple steps have results that seem magical such as looking at self honestly, without judgment or criticism, or fear of rebuke. Discovering why you want a certain payoff, looking at it honestly and then finding a healthier way to achieve the same result is so empowering—self-worth soars. Life finally feels good.

Can We Be Hexed?

While doing tarot readings at a psychic fair in Canada, I was assigned a space surrounded by several booths run by members of a close-knit cultural group. They charged less than I did, advertised themselves differently and projected a mystical, secretive style in their readings; all the things I try to discourage in mine. Their dress was fun, bizarre, and colorful, definitely not mainstream. I generated a lot of business but they didn't, even at their rock bottom prices. I sensed jealousy—they wouldn't chat with me and there seemed to be a lot of focused ignoring of me. "Oh well," I thought, "I'm here to work."

By the middle of the second day, the situation was worse. Then a truly bizarre woman, an associate of theirs I had seen in their booths, walked into mine, loudly proclaiming, "Dolly Mae, Dolly Mae. Well, Dolly Mae, I'm going to have a reading from you," and sat down.

This was her first attempt at intimidation. She didn't want the reading taped, which was odd, and said I should be flattered she'd chosen me. Her whole attitude was condescending and false.

As the session began, I felt something going on at a different level. It began with her odd conduct about paying me up front and in secret so that "her aunt in the next booth wouldn't see." She told me to quickly hide the money. This was an attempt at control. If I had followed her "orders," she would have instantly known that she could manipulate me. I responded that if her aunt had a problem it was her aunt's problem and that she was free to make her own choices. An odd sort of mind-game began. She was attempting to intimidate me to prove her power and to make me feel afraid. I clearly represented a challenge.

Her reading was about her being two different people-one presented to the outside world, the other kept hidden within, fearful of being ridiculed. It was her soft side that was hidden, while outwardly she presented a strong, intense side. She greatly feared vulnerability.

During the reading, she told me that she was a witch and a high priestess. She wanted to impress me and to create fear, so she embellished her story. I told her that I was familiar with witches of the earthy Wicca religion and had no problem with that. The final card in the Tarot reading was The Devil card. She pointed to it telling me, "Whenever this card comes up in a reading, it means an evil spirit." She said this pointedly and threateningly, as though she knew a secret.

I said, "It does if you believe it does, and for you it may. But for me it means an unhealthy attachment to something that is physically bad for you, probably your lover," whom we were already discussing.

She was obviously used to creating victims but I wasn't taking the bait. She tried to convince me of the evil spirit, but her game wasn't working. In the course of the reading, she had said, "I'm using you to see through your eyes," another power play. This was supposed to engender fear in me. Instead I thought, *how clever, to use generated psychic energy between two people to create greater vision. This is as it should be.* I was not in fear that "she was inside my head" or that she might have greater powers than I. My belief is that two are more powerful than one as in the old Bible saying, "Where two or more are gathered ..."

During the session, she asked a question, to which I responded, "It's similar to the two conversations that are going on simultaneously between you and me. One is spoken, the other is unspoken."

At this, she flared up, threw herself back from the table and shouted, "I'm not doing anything!"

But indeed she was. She had been running a constant dialogue with me on an unspoken level, totally coherent, but in an effort to control me, sidetrack me and create fear. It was a strange experience and was the more meaningful of the two conversations. It held the deeper truths about her. She was so fear-based that she knew only victim-persecutor games. The fact that she had reacted so violently validated my observation and put her on notice that I was consciously aware of her game and still not afraid of her. Then the unspoken second conversation stopped and her games ended.

Later that night, my roommate and I discussed the session and concluded the woman's group had held a ritual ceremony to "hex" me because they felt threatened by my success. We then tied into their arcane ceremony and the potion they had concocted "in my honor." I was unaffected. All of it seemed fear-based to me. I didn't feel the need to accept their ritual and therefore felt no need to repel it or defend against it.

I had always wondered what would happen if I were the target of a voodoo curse or something similar. Is it really real? Does it take not only a sender, but a receptive receiver? This seemed to prove I was right. Since I hold to self-empowerment concepts, I was not a player in that arena.

At that time, I was working my way through *A Course In Miracles*. I was on the lesson "You Already Are As God Created You," which contains the following helpful text:

"... nothing can be added to nor subtracted from you,
    because you already are as God created you."

So no one could add a hex onto me, nor remove any ability I might possess. I already am as God created me, nothing more nor less. No one could "do it to me."

This experience put me in bliss with the depths of awareness I had achieved. I was laughing and crying all at once at the deep joy this knowing created. I instantly experienced and confirmed the safety of the universe. There was absolutely no doubt in me at all.

I now know that voodoo hexing really is an exercise in co-created fear. It takes two fearful beings to make it work, a fear-based sender and a fear-based receiver. We must play in the Triangle of Fear, seeing ourselves alternately as a victim and then needing to gain control as a persecutor. If we hold onto love, knowing we are its source, we can't be affected. It is only that part of us that fears an unsafe universe and perceives itself as a victim or potential victim. Only then could we participate in a "successful" hexing. In my case I chose love and joy, not fear. Therefore I could not be hexed, and was only positively affected. I could only feel deep and intense love for all those who had participated in the experience of such a gift to me.

The next morning at the fair, all those from the group came up to my booth individually, each asking me the same exact question: "How was your night?"

I was grinning from ear-to-ear and responded each time with, "Wonderful. Thank you!" or "Marvelous! Thank you!" emphasizing and personalizing 'you' as an acknowledgment of their participation in my gift. From that day on, I was included in their group and never again treated as an outsider. I had passed some test in their minds. They brought food gifts to me, such as home-baked goodies. They asked favors. They shared experiences and personal parts of their lives. I learned to see them differently, as they had learned to see me. By mid-morning, my cheeks hurt from the intense grin, and I must have glowed from joy. I *knew* I already was as God created me.

Lawsuit

A close family member has recently served us with a rather sizeable lawsuit. Now a crisis looms, personal and intimate. It is present and palpable. We have many options. We can become gripped by fear. We can choose victimhood and become defensive and righteous, venting frustration at perceived injustice and lining up family members on opposing sides. We can thrash in the fear. The real question is, as always, who and what do I choose to be in this drama? What is my highest thought about myself and the role I choose to play? Am I willing to embrace it? Can I allow myself to feel the pain of being a creator in this drama? Can I acknowledge it as real, honor both the plaintiff's pain and mine, and let go? Who am I in relationship to this experience? Where is my focus? I know I will get more of what I focus on. Who do I choose to be?

I choose love. I will always choose love. I will send love, allow love, create love, know love and be love. I will use love to heal any sense of victimhood remaining within me. All my experiences are about the self. Yes, there are triggers and other actors on my stage, but I brought them into my world to help me move past my fears. I will remember the perfection of all things, walking in the light and allowing. I will acknowledge that I am the creator of my own experiences and that this is merely a reflection of what I have not yet healed or loved. I will remember to thank my protagonist, my trigger, for he has done me a great service by bringing me this opportunity to remember to be the highest expression of who and what I am. I will not hang on to any particular outcome. I will allow it all. I will know that my highest and best good is served by aligning with my highest consciousness, which always holds the focus of love.

Opportunities for victimhood are real. They are always just around the corner. They may be large or small. It is not the action or trigger that is the important focus but how we respond that makes all the difference in our world. Look at those words: "all the difference in our world." I know that even my small choices can add to the sum of joy and love, or of fear and hate in consciousness.

We now get to choose how to be in relationship to this fear. We can feed the fear or move through it and past it. So we choose to see this as an opportunity to process any remaining money fears, to align with an abundant universe and know that abundance is ours. If we stay stuck in fear of lack, then we are part of the old fear paradigm.

We will not hold this person in our consciousness in anger or fear. Instead we will hold him and his fears in the more powerful energy of love, not to change him or to serve any particular outcome, but to see him as perfect, no matter what his actions. He can only act from the highest state of who he is in this now. To change is his choice. We will do this for ourselves because love is how we heal ourselves and, in doing so, our planet. I choose to create peace and love no matter what the triggers may first awaken in me. I stop, realize I am a creator, not a victim, feel my emotions of fear, anger or frustration fully, then step back and choose to feel love. War stops here, now, with me.

Child Abuse

No matter what the perceived injury, the following precepts still hold true:

- Judge not, lest you be judged.
- Love others as you love yourself.
- Turn the other cheek. This isn't done so you can be abused again. This is to prove to others that they have not injured you. This shows them that you are not a victim and that when you turn the other cheek you are offering them the opportunity to choose again to act in love.
- You can choose how to respond.

Abuse has existed ever since fear first entered our reality. Sexual molestation is a deeply personal violation, deserving of great compassion, for both the victim and the persecutor. Why does God, in his or her infinite love, wisdom and compassion, not see fit to step in and stop these situations? Could it be that our higher awareness knows that no one involved is truly a victim, but that we are all creators? God allows everything without judgment, knowing that neither the abuser nor the abused is "broken". There is no excuse for such abuse, yet there is always a reason for it. Until we have lived in the minds and hearts of both the victims and molesters, who are we to know? Each person chooses his own highest path as he/she perceives it, no matter how offensive it may seem to others.

At some point, a pearl of wisdom in all the fear and victimization will be revealed. Many people are affected by a single abuse situation and, for each, the essence of the teaching that comes with seeking a higher knowing will be different. For the families and friends of both the abused and the abuser, there are different awarenesses. Each realizes vulnerability, fear, and a whole range of emotions that either catalyze more fear or more understanding. The choice is clear at that point. All the same principles we have discussed in this book still apply, even here.

Each small act adds to the sum total of planetary awakening and ultimately serves to shift mass consciousness beyond victimization. A great number of people have been sexually molested and there is enormous resistance to giving up their victimhood. Everyone has a choice about how they respond to events. Everyone is a creator. This is not to say that they did it to themselves and therefore deserve it. Not at all. Do not remain in your limited human perspective and hold on to the hurt and pain of molestation. Honor each one's choices as a grand and glorious spirit inhabiting a physical body on its soul's business. This is a creation from one's highest self, an opportunity to grow spiritually … or not. Choose to see molestation from your higher spiritual perspective that judges not.

With each discovery of past or current molestation, a new opportunity arises to decide who and what we are in relationship to it. Will we continue to play the victim role? It may serve us to surrender into that space for a while to be nurtured, to fill a void and help heal ourselves. I do not suggest that we ignore such an emotionally overwhelming event. Simply be aware that we can choose to move past the pain or remain stuck in it, re-wounding ourselves over and over, adding to the world's sum total of pain, hurt and victimhood. Or we can surmount it, move through the pain, choose joy, select a different path and know we ourselves create our lives. Ask what opportunity this experience brings us, and get on with a new and different path of awareness and enlightenment.

What possible perspective can we use to understand molestation? We do not give infants and children credit for being spiritual or for being individually aware souls. However they are more connected with their Godself than most adults. They are infinitely closer to their remembrance of who they really are.

Consider this perspective. We each choose to come into this reality. We actually choose the genetics we will use as the vehicle to our soul's journey. We construct and create the general pattern of our lives. These may be emotionally rich, short-lived, gifted, physically challenged, mundane and calm, challenging, spiritually handicapped or highly intuitive. Once we enter this world, we pass through the veil of forgetfulness and lose our remembrance of our plan, our choices and our lofty desires for spiritual awaking in this physical form. However, once we set out on a conscious path to awaken and remember, we learn that we are creators here and now. We learn that we are not victims of our intentions prior to entering our physical form. We learn we can choose differently, shift our life pattern and get off the karmic wheel, that is, the wheel of *unconsciously chosen experience*. Once we own that we create our paths, we can literally create a whole different reality from the plan *we* selected when we entered this one. There is no predestined divine plan for us, no single main purpose for our individual lives except:

- TO EXPERIENCE
- TO BE IN JOY, and
- TO REMEMBER WHO WE ARE.

We have set out so many opportunities (challenges) for ourselves to awaken, to remember, to shift, to grow, to know who and what we are. Why then would we interfere with and judge the path taken by others? How could we possibly know their journey better than they? How can we judge? Each of us follows his/her own internal guidance and must determine its source as God or ego. This is determined by the vibration, feeling and value of the guidance and whether it is based on love or fear. This is why it is so important to develop our feeling center, our gut, so we will recognize the source of the information we receive; to validate it is of the highest vibration. This is the higher path of discernment, not judgment.

SIDS (Sudden Infant Death Syndrome)

Consider this. All beings have free will. Each soul entering this plane of existence develops a body little-by-little. In the process of aging, we become emotionally withdrawn and resistant, mentally more stuck, physically more dense and attached to our bodies, unless we choose how to think, feel and live consciously. The newly embodied being moves further away from remembrance of its Godself. While still in our highly aware spirit form, our more conscious soul state, each of us made contractual agreements with others who would be in our play upon life's stage with us. Most of us have been here before and are reincarnated in this new body to have once again an opportunity to experience the great "Aha!" in remembering who we really are. However, we could only have this awakening "Aha!" if we put on the veil of forgetfulness upon entering this realm.

Those pre-life contractual agreements may have occurred like this: You say to another dear soul in spirit form, "You go down first and be the mom this time. I did it last time. But I don't want to get stuck in all that earth stuff again. It's so enticing and powerful. I want to feel what it's like again to be connected with a physical body, but this time I want to stay for just a short while, so please have an abortion when I'm in your womb."

Of course, the other angelic soul agrees, saying, "Yes, of course. Just please remember why we are doing this and at the moment of your earthly release, remember who we are and how we have assisted each other on our chosen journeys."

In another case, one soul may have said, "I'm not going to stay long in the physical body. I just want to be there for a brief time, so you be the mom and then I'm going to leave some time within the first couple of years."

"Great!" exclaims the mother-to-be. "I also look forward to the intense emotional journey of such an experience. I also will benefit greatly from this life's passage. But I'll try to remember that we have both agreed to this and see it as the handiwork of creation and experience the love of seeing you off on your journey back here."

Contracts made. Forgetfulness reins. Life stirs. Abortion and SIDS death occur. Emotions experienced. Contract completed. Growth achieved. Human emotions, judgment, anger, mass consciousness, others stepping in our path's way, disempowerment and, voila, a victim extraordinaire. We simply forgot. A fetus and an infant have free will, too. In fact, they are closer to remembering who they are than we adults are. Their spiritual selves are more intact. Their contracts are more felt than thought. Things make emotional sense to them because they are love-based. They also will make sense to us as adults when we become love-based.

Loss of a Child

This is one of the most difficult emotional hurdles in life. We can endure pain, financial loss, divorce, illness and emotional crisis; everything is relative to the innocence that appears to be violated. Again we have forgotten our pre-life contractual agreements made while in spirit form. Remember, all deaths are, in truth, suicides, self-created. They are not punishments from God.

These decisions rarely come from the conscious mind. Instead they are part of the higher self. They may result from the wounded self ending its pain or having had enough of its earthly journey or carelessly judging the value of the experience of putting on a body and coming to earth. Life may also be ended because it is time for that soul to go forward to a more awakened state of being in a different reality, a different form or dimension. We are not the only beings in the universe. We might as well believe the Earth is still flat.

Many people have had angelic and spirit guide contact. In fact, there have been far too many of these experiences to ignore. Near death experiences abound with proofs for those who are open. Past lives come to light with irrefutable evidence to shed light on our past. Many people channel enlightened spiritual beings of love from higher vibrations who verify the existence of other worlds and other realities.

The point we seem to miss is that it is the *spiritual self* making these choices out of remembrance of who it really is and what it chooses to do next. When we understand that children are also highly developed spiritual beings, we will stop blaming God for their deaths. They too chose, from their higher state. We can bless them and support them in their decision and honor it. They have not abandoned us, nor we them. They have not intended to cause us pain. In their highest state they also know that we are each responsible for our own feelings. Other people are but triggers. Such children have simply chosen to return to a different form of their closeness with God and Love. How could we dishonor that choice? Our grief and loss is real. So is their joy.

The trauma of such overwhelming crisis may be overcome through counseling, prayer, understanding and faith in an unconditionally loving God. Those of us who assist others in such grief must remain compassionate, allowing and loving. We can remember their perfection for them, know their journey is arduous, but perfect, and allow their process. Although they grieve, they are not broken and neither do they need to be fixed. Life, grief and love are processes. It is up to us how we move through them.

9/11/01

On September 11, 2001, the terrorists struck. The entire world was overwhelmed and numbed by pain, sorrow, frustration, and grief. All these feelings are real. Our hearts go out to all who have been impacted by this tragic and terrible event. Now is the time for choice. A great offering is now before human consciousness. By our choice, we see who we are at our very core. Who do we choose to be? Will we choose compassion or revenge?

There is no denying that the September 11th attack was a horrific and terrifying act on the part of terrorists. When we judge an event, we have chosen to stop the flow and refuse to allow the unfolding of a grander vision of the events in their proper perspective. Ask yourself, "What if this undeniably impacting event has changed our consciousness, forever lifting it up, propelling us into a love-based God-aligned Consciousness?"

We can stop our judgment and seek instead how this event could hold the seed of benefit. As we so seek, we cannot fail to see that each person acts from his or her highest self-perspective and cannot do otherwise. The terrorists are acting out of their understanding of God and love. When will we see we are all one? There is only one God with many faces.

Wars are for the purpose of economic gain and the increase of power, regardless of how lofty the original impetus seems to be. They are fueled by the manipulation of the unprocessed emotional energy of the public. Leaders mold public opinion to serve their own ends. It is up to us to make our own decisions by listening to what is in our hearts and seeing our highest image of ourselves. Our fear of feeling is the root of hatred, anger and revenge. At what cost will we continue to push aside our ability to touch into the depths of our own pain and strike out in vengeful victimhood?

Revenge leads clearly to victim consciousness and the dark oppression of fear. The path of compassion adds to the sum total of light and love in the universe. If we touch into the feelings of others but resist moving into the depths of our own feelings, it is because we fear being overwhelmed. To avoid feeling the intensity of our own grief, our loss of feeling safe and our shock, we divert this energy into a need to *do* something, to react. In some way revenge becomes an option. Violence and reaction are for those who have shoved aside *feeling* their own pain. It is a choice. Revenge feels very active, yet it only adds to the world's sum total of pain.

Our greatest danger is in losing our compassion for the terrorists by separating ourselves from them and making them an "it." It is so easy to become emotionally distraught and manipulated by media into hating an "it." They become the enemy, dehumanized, and a focal point for all our own unresolved fears. We can easily buy into and own victimhood consciousness.

There is always a higher perspective. We can choose to see with our limited human victim perspective or from our spiritual self that knows all things are parts of a whole and that love is the highest experience. Love is what is lacking in this world, love of self, first. In loving ourselves completely, we heal the world. By embracing the other's experience of fear as well as our own, we make the world an "us." Can we choose to find the part of ourselves that brings terror to us? It is that part of us that has not yet been loved and fears the light. We can then love our terror into wholeness.

The constant input from the media numbs our minds. Why? Because it keeps us caught in the dynamics of thrashing. We become ensnared in living the daily soap operas pressures of goals and fears, trapped in their webs. Reading or watching the news keeps our minds wrapped in fear through observing, discussing and being in awe of victims, rescuers and persecutors. All this thrashing about diverts us and keeps us numbed to our own inner feelings and guidance.

We constantly seek new and more amazing input. This becomes a craving. We end up addicted to the viewpoints of the editors, the newsmen and mass media. We are being emotionally manipulated and tune in for more and more.

It is a choice to allow this to continue. Our televisions and radios have off buttons. The choice of programming is ours. We can think for ourselves. We can quiet the external information sources and allow inner guidance to surface. Our feelings are ours to guide and mold so we can just sit quietly and feel. We can allow our own understanding to evolve separate from mass media driven consciousness. Who is going to give us permission to learn from ourselves? Who is going to teach us how to think for ourselves? We are. It is a choice.

As we become more conscious, more light-filled, we have constant choice before us. Who will we be? What would love do? Compassion is feeling another's pain, acknowledging it, validating it for them, knowing it is real, and honoring it as their journey. Empathy is choosing to take their path with them and losing ourselves in it. If a funeral director were to grieve along with each group of mourners, he would be totally ineffective in supporting the bereaved in each subsequent funeral. So, too, the leaders of the world must validate the pain of others, experience their own and hold the space of love for all those affected. A leader can choose to lead into a better way of being, a higher sense of self. An enlightened leader will find a way to resolve, defuse, include, align and add love to the world.

When we can love the neighbor down the street whose barking dog awakens us, whose unmuffled car speeds past our house, or whose home is painted "quaintly," then we will put an end to war. War does not start "out there," but "in here," with each judgment we make about our own family members, our neighbors, our friends, our town and our daily life. In this crisis, we get to make the most important choice of our lives. Who will we choose to be? A source of love or fear? What energy will we choose to add to? We can hold the high watch for peace. One person can change the world for good or bad: bin Laden, Christ, Gandhi, Buddha, Hitler, the Dalai Lama or You. Who are you? Will you choose love or fear?

How Do We Deal With Hate?

What do we do with it? Where do we put it? How do we direct it if we hate terrorists? We can choose. Do we wish to participate in revenge or compassion? Who is it we will decide to become? What is in our highest view of ourselves? Killing? Guilt? Blame? If a few terrorists can create an emotional upheaval, then those of us holding the space for Light can choose to redirect that energy to create love. The hate we may feel is a reflection of hate we feel towards ourselves. **What we judge in others is always what we have not yet learned to love in ourselves.** It is so easy to galvanize others together against something. We stand together *against* poverty, against disease, against terrorism. Do we stand together *for* love?

Fear runs deep. It is easier to get people to take action against poverty, disease and terrorism because they fear it for themselves. It is easier because people believe that their value is in *doing* something instead of *being* something. She/he who chooses to *be* a source of love appears to *do* nothing. One might as well say that in mathematics the zero is worthless because it is nothing. However, it is the ultimate space-holder. By doing nothing, it performs an invaluable function. The world of mathematics could not exist without this extraordinary nothing. I think we would all like just a few zeros in our bank balance, perhaps only 10 measly zeros! Ten space-holders! Ten people who don't react. Ten nothings can't mean much, or can they? Think about your value in holding the space for love and joy. This is not about resistance. This is about choice, about your choosing between a state of being versus a state of doing.

Conclusion

Love is who we are. As the world shifts into a new vibration, our real self emerges and compels our awakening. Each moment becomes an opportunity to step into and align with our higher selves. Choosing joy in the midst of crisis is achieved by choosing what love would do now and following the path that love offers.

We *can* choose joy. It's always an option.

Appendix: The Soul Speaks

The Soul Speaks, found on the next two pages, is a collection of sayings that I use, refer to and teach. Many came from my beloved teacher, Rajni. Many are original. All are ancient truths, applicable to everyday situations.

Each one has layer upon layer underlying its apparently simplistic wisdom. But isn't it that the way with simple truths. I hope you will find these sayings useful in your meditations, prayers and thoughts.

Choose Joy, Drink Water and Stay in the Now.

The Universe is always willing to rearrange itself for you.

Power exists only in the now.

Argue for your limitations and you get to keep them.

Judgment is what you haven't yet learned to love about yourself.

What you resist persists.

If you would judge, Love your judgment.

Judgment stops the flow.

Choosing fear is placing something else above God; for if you would choose God, you would choose only Love.

What you deny, resist or defend *is* your issue.

What you focus on you get more of.

'Shoulds' are how you die the body.

Those who speak to you in limitation are not coming from their godself.

Anger, Hate, Fear? Tear the label off and it's just raw energy.

"I am ..." statements are powerfully creative.

Fear is only one choice.

I don't love you in spite of our differences; I love you because of them.

Love your fears to death.

Choose Joy! It's always an option.

About the Author

Dolly Mae was a successful investment business owner for 20 years, teaching thousands how to succeed financially until it all collapsed during a nightmare $25 million bankruptcy. In asking, "Why is this happening?" she found answers that apply to all of life's challenges.

Integrating business and intuition, she teaches growth and empowerment through worldwide lectures and private consultations in the US, Egypt, Bali, Greece, Peru and Canada. She is a frequent guest on TV and talk radio. She currently lives near Seattle, WA with her life mate, Jim Jenkins.

Dolly can be contacted at 1 877 CHOZ JOY (246-9569), by email at dolly@dollymae.com or via her website: www.dollymae.com.

Order Form

QTY.		US	CDN	Total
	Choosing Joy in the Midst of Crisis by Dolly Mae	$17.95	$27.95	
SHIPPING AND HANDLING　　　Global Priority: $7.50 USA: $4.95 for first book ordered/$3.00 each additional book				
SALES TAX (WA state residents only, add 8.9%)				
Total enclosed				

Telephone Orders:
Call 1-800-461-1931
Have your VISA or
Mastercard ready.

Fax Orders:
425-398-1380
Complete this order
form, and fax.

Postal Orders:
Hara Publishing
PO Box 19732
Seattle, WA 98109

E-mail Orders:
harapub@foxinternet.net

Method of Payment:

❑ Check or Money Order

❑

❑

Expiration Date: _____

Card #: _____

Signature: _____

Name_____
Address_____
City_____ State_____ ZIP_____
Phone ( )_____ Fax ( )_____